HOUSE, PRECINCT, TERRITORY

DESIGN STRATEGIES FOR THE PRODUCTIVE CITY

Graham Crist
John Doyle
Rafael Luna
Silvia Micheli
Antony Moulis
Dongwoo Yim

UQ School of Architecture, Brisbane

Dr Silvia Micheli

Associate Professor
Antony Moulis

Dr Peyman Akhgar

Contact:
Jocks Rd, St Lucia
QLD 4067 AUSTRALIA

Phone: +617 3365 3537
Email: adp@uq.edu.au

RMIT University School of Architecture & Urban Design

Dr John Doyle

Associate Professor Graham Crist

Contact:
RMIT Building 100

Swanston Street, Carlton
VIC 3053 AUSTRALIA

Phone: +613 9925 1010
Email: aud.he@rmit.com.au

PRAUD

Dr Rafael Luna

Dongwoo Yim

Contact:
서울시 성동구 광나루로4길 13

13 Gwangnaruro 4 Gil
Seoul, S.Korea [04054]

Phone: +82 2 3144 1226
Phone: +613 9925 1010
Email: info@praud.info

Supported by:

PRAUD

CONTENTS

IMAGINE A CITY WHERE YOU CAN WALK TO A FACTORY JOB IN YOUR NEIGHBOURHOOD, KNOW YOUR CO-WORKERS, HAVE A SUPPORTIVE COMMUNITY, AND TAKE PRIDE IN YOUR OWN CRAFTSMANSHIP AND HANDWORK—MAKING THINGS FOR BOTH A LOCAL AND GLOBAL ECONOMY THAT IS SELF-SUFFICIENT AT THE CITY SCALE IN A NEW URBAN PARADIGM. WHILE THIS MAY SOUND SLIGHTLY NOSTALGIC AND IDEALISTIC, THE LACK OF ATTENTION TO PHYSICAL PRODUCTION SPACES, NOW OFTEN COMMUNITY-BASED RATHER THAN THAT OF CAPITALIST PRODUCTION, HAS GAINED INTEREST IN THE FIELD OF URBAN DESIGN AND ARCHITECTURE. THIS HAS INSPIRED NEW FORMS FOR ECONOMIC DEVELOPMENT AND URBAN PLANNING, FOCUSING THE ATTENTION ON MAINTAINING BOTH LARGE AND SMALL SPACES FOR INDUSTRIES AND TRANSFORMING THEM INTO DIVERSE HYBRID SPACES.

Since I began teaching (seminars on industrial history and co-teaching the studio Vertical Urban Factory, in 2006 which led to an eponymous traveling exhibition and book in 2015),[1] curatorial and consulting practice, my focus has remained constant in investigating methods for encouraging manufacturing at various scales in cities. Maintaining local production provides much needed jobs, equitable and diverse opportunities, and sustainable industrial eco-systems. In investigating today's issues in urban production, the themes outlined in Vertical Urban Factory of the sustainable, the flexible, the spectacle as the "consumption of production,"[2] the hybrid, and the new industrial commons,[3] became essential for the future of production of things in cities.

The hybrid aspect, and its potential, sustained my current scholarship leading to the book, Hybrid Factory/Hybrid City (2023),[4] comprised of a series of essays based on a symposium in Turin (pre COVID-19) when the idea of "the hybrid" workplace was barely a concept—as a way to integrate light, clean, green, and quiet production processes for economic resilience while rethinking zoning, building code, and environmental issues for a circular economy.

We posed questions such as how can we develop cities to include new factory paradigms now that production in the new economy is clean, quiet, and small-scale? What kinds of hybrid mixes can we make in our cities that include industrial uses? How can these spaces encourage new entrepreneurs, jobs, and economic equity along with viable urban forms?

How do we break the planning and land-use patterns of segregated zoning by class and function and encourage mixed-use zoning? If the hybrid refers to the infusion of not only programs but also their infrastructure, structure, and form then what are these initially assumed properties that are thrown into the mix?

The unpredicted effect of dividing industry from other uses, sequestering them beyond, even the hinterlands, to other country's Export Processing Zones, resulted in horrible living and working conditions. Manufacturing as separated from daily urban life through zoning codes, segregated not only the work process but also the workers from city life and from the public view, resulting in the homogenized zoning of cities, a process that often stagnates economic growth, as observed by David Harvey and Jane Jacobs.[5] The hybrid mixed-use factory and district could thus make for a more flexible and dynamic city with a strong industrial eco-system with a shorter supply chain as well as one that is dense or "tight" as the authours here discuss. Cities and new advanced production methods are sustainable and we see both the hybrid and the "vertical urban factory" reinforcing those goals. Mixing creates opportunities, random encounters, and entrepreneurship builds community and self-directed production. By separating activities from one another, we have also learned from COVID-19 that we do need things in proximity, in what we call a "16-minute city," inclusive of industry,[6] to enhance our ability to express ourselves, have positive health, and move from one place of expression to another as a potent value for life.

In this book—House, Precinct, Territory: Design Strategies for the Productive City—the speculative projects parallel ideas to activate and relish productive spaces in Brisbane, Seoul, and Melbourne—with individualised economic, social, political, building, zoning, and environmental concerns. However, what links them all is the common interest of where to place production, what form it should take, and how to make it re-adjust and question the norm of zoning and building codes, while ensuring the workplaces are safe, secure, and sustainable. These codes and regulations simultaneously provide organisational and performative zoning opportunities for integration of uses and changes in normative planning practices. The interests in those aspects all directly intertwine with economics in cities to supply jobs to those who are in need at local and global regions—the "global" scale. These issues are reflective, creating a renewed dynamism that is trans-disciplinary; they merge, cross through agencies and issues as city administrations struggle with health, safety, and how to add human value to production rather than extract it, as economist Mariana Mazzucato argues.[7]

The three main investigations presented in this volume relate to many current questions in production spatial practice, focusing on the home and neighbourhood, adaptation of buildings to maintain productive density in a district, and urban food production resources at the larger scale.

The home has always been a place of production both of reproductive labor and that of making things.[8] It is a space that primarily centers around the production by women—cooking, cleaning, providing emotional support, and as mothers, producing children who in turn must be productive. Historically, in numerous indigenous cultures, women produced goods for the home that continued during the first Industrial Revolution with cottage industries, which included entire families producing goods that a middleman would then sell in the marketplace, mixing uses prior to Euclidian zoning. Even garages, or the boîte, in French, as ad hoc and informal spaces, continue to be the site of major experimentation such as in Philadelphia, where the first computer was invented. In the first study in this book, "House", set in Brisbane, these projects for neo-cottage industries show how designs beyond the yard, the sidewalk, and the garage sale can configure the buying and selling of goods by opening the traditional suburban fence as a new porous space for artisanal production and community interaction.

The interest in density as a solution to urban manufacturing is also referential to the ideas presented in Vertical Urban Factory, both as a building typology that organizes structure and serves as a metaphor for urban production spaces that rise tall in multistoried buildings and has extracted the significance of the early twentieth century urban loft factory. The reuse of these factories as industrial spaces can most easily contribute to the expansion and retention of production in a denser city. The vertical urban factory gained traction with its smaller urban footprint inspiring collaborations and invention. Its proximity to residences reduces the worker's commute and thus the carbon footprint of both the factory and the worker. Contingent to urban locations is the larger employment pool for both skilled and unskilled workers that then provides additional incentives for factories to expand in cities.

The density of these vertical factories is orchestrated through mechanisms such as elevators, spiral chutes, vertical conveyors, and mechanical systems that are either integrated or attached as clip-ons to factories at later dates.[9] This is evident in Hong Kong with its high-rise factories with exterior ductwork and interchangeable parts. Here, in the study of "Precinct" of Seoul's industrial and more generic buildings adapted with mechanical and Heating, Ventilation, and Air Conditioning (HVAC) systems, spatial additions, signage and plug-ins become external parasites in synergy with the numerous loft-type buildings. How can we learn from these adaptations for the future of the flexible buildings and the city? How can we take advantage of this type and construction method to respond to what is there and exists as "the found," in terms of Alison and Peter Smithson[10] and harness the design and technical capabilities of these functional forms that are both high-tech and Brutalist in their adhocism of design?

Ideas for vertical urban farms are often discussed as ways to improve the urban food supply chain, as Dickson Despommier and MVRDV have instigated and now exist globally.[11] While the costs are high for the quantity produced and the small scale of entrepreneurs, including Vertical Harvest in Jackson Hole or the Floating Farm in Rotterdam, these experiments contribute to closed-loop production systems that need a great deal of traction and proof of concept. In the section "Territory" set in Melbourne, a future imaginary explores how growing food in cities can contribute to self-sufficiency but has to be scaled up to feed an entire city showing the drawbacks and challenges with the invention. Intense data analysis and growing systems information provides a backbone to the study that could be established in numerous cities. With the current interest in buying authentic and locally produced things, there is a rise in the consumers' power and the importance of corporate transparency that the vertical urban farm could provoke how and where we get our food, while also increasing a city's compactness.

As urban factories survive at a smaller scale, making products that are nimbler with advanced manufacturing changing zoning and building codes, design and the environment need to be more flexible, while following environmental regulations. In this book, we see further investigations into new forms of industries for a dynamic urbanism that contributes to diversity, mixity, and vitality in new, rarely imagined, closed-loop systems that can focus on performative measures open to flux. As we change the types of manufacturing, our spaces need to change, and city policy needs to respond quickly to accommodate them.

If we can provide a place where people can earn a living, often with little training or experience in industrial jobs, a new paradigm in a circular economy for a sustainable future is possible. The community of production, whether it be in the home as domestic production, the neighborhood and precinct or the territory, has potential as spaces for diversification that adapt. As Lefebvre emphasizes, "...while at the same time the relative importance attached to functional distinctions disappears. Appropriate places would be fixed, semi-fixed, movable or vacant,"[12] as seen in some new multi-use projects that include industrial use. This will point towards a new urban manifestation and a more open, dynamic, equitable, and just city as creating spaces that combine not segregate, their essential needs for working, playing, and living. As the authors in this book correctly present—this reevaluation of the factory's spatial typology, its ecology, and economic potential allow for an increase in mixes at each scale from that of the building to the district or neighborhood that is dispersed throughout the entire city.

Endnotes

1. See Nina Rappaport, Vertical Urban Factory, Barcelona, Actar, 2015 and soft edition 2020. The exhibition began at the Skyscraper Museum, New York City in 2010 and has traveled to thirteen venues including Brussels in 2022 and Rotterdam most recently in 2023.
2. See Nina Rappaport, "The Consumption of Production," Praxis, Columbia University, 2003.
3. See Nina Rappaport, "The New Industrial Commons," in AD: Productive Urbanism, Eds. Dongwoo Yim and Rafael Luna, London, 2021.
4. Nina Rappaport, Ed., Hybrid Factory/Hybrid City, (Actar 2022) includes essays by Nina Rappaport, Bram Aerts (TRANS architectuur | stedenbouw), Frank Barkow (Barkow Leibinger Architects), Cristina Bianchetti (Politecnico di Torino), Giovanna Fossa (Politecnico di Milano), Nicholas Gilliland (Tollila + Gilliland Atelier), Dieter Leyssen and Eva de Bruyn (51N4E), Nicola Russi (Politecnico di Torino and Laboratorio Permanente), Matteo Robiglio (Politecnico di Torino and TRA), Maria Paola Repellino (Politecnico di Torino), Markus Schâefer (Hosoya Schâefer Architects), Giulia Setti (Politecnico di Milano), Ward Verbakel (plusoffice architects), Ianira Vassallo (Politecnico di Torino), and Juan Lucas Young (Sauerbruch Hutton).
5. See both David Harvey, The Condition of Postmodernity: An Enquiry into the Origins of Cultural Change, Cambridge Mass: Blackwell Publishing, 1990 and Jane Jacobs, The Economy of Cities, New York: Vintage Books, 1969.
6. Hybrid Factory Hybrid City, roundtable discussion, pp. 247-249.
7. See Mariana Mazzucato, The Value of Everything, New York: Public Affairs, 2018.
8. Pier Vittorio Aureli and Maria S. Giudici, "Familiar Horror: Toward a Critique of Domestic Space," Log No. 38, 2016
9. Rob Lane in Lane and Rappaport, Eds., " ARTICLE NAME HERE," Design of Urban Manufacturing, New York: Routledge, 2020.
10. Alison and Peter Smithson discuss the idea of the "as found" as looking at what is there, essay by Dirk van den Heuvel, As Found: The Metamorphosis of the Everyday. On the Work of Nigel Henderson, Eduardo Paolozzi, and Alison and Peter Smithson (1953-1956). Scratching the Surface, OASE, (59), 52–67, 2002.
11. See Dickson Despommier, The Vertical Farm, Thomas Dunne Books, 2010.
12. Henri Lefebvre, The Production of Space, Cambridge, Mass: Blackwell Publishing, 1991, p. 363.

PROPOSITIONS FOR URBAN PRODUCTION

In architecture and urban design, a productive city is defined as an entity combining living and the making of goods. Production within cities is not a new phenomenon. In the centuries before the industrial revolution, cities were already productive. It was only after the industrial revolution and the gradual advancement of modern technologies from the 19th century that the normative ways cities functioned were challenged. House, Precinct, Territory: Design Strategies for the Productive City develops scenario-based design models for possible urban futures, rethinking the relationships between working and living.

The contemporary city has predominantly become a place of consumption, as it is understood through western and dominant global planning frameworks. Over the last 150 years, the productive capacity of cities has progressively dwindled and been dispersed. From the late 19th century, modernist urban planners, such as Ebenezer Howard, Le Corbusier, and Clarence Stein, criticised the dense structure and appearance of existing cities. The traditional city was deemed unfit to accommodate modern factories and new technologies and was perceived as a place of "overcrowding, noise, dirt, crime, poverty, and disease"[1], not the result of a purposeful plan. An anti-density agenda emerged, basing its theories on abstract rules and regulations, encouraging functional division and sprawl as a guideline for designing the future city.

The emerging mechanised trends and demands of large-scale industries and retail operations gradually led to the marginalisation of productive sites away from city centres and spaces of living. This intentional division was exacerbated by the implementation of single-use zoning. Originally known as Euclidean zoning, this approach gained popularity after use of the automobile became widespread in the early 20th century, which allowed for transit between distance-separating land parcels. The modern city was divided into separate parcels of land, assigned to distinct uses and activities, such as commercial, residential, industrial, and recreational areas, leaving most production sites located away from city centres.

Technology enabled the conception of dispersed cities. Frank Lloyd Wright's Broadacre City, exhibited in 1934, proposed the total diffusion of city by providing each resident with an acre of land where individuals could independently manage agricultural production. The 1951 CIAM 8 event The Heart of the City proved to be critical of this dispersion when Josep Lluís Sert reconsidered the civic core as essential for the survival of modern cities. The dualities between dispersion and tightening, zoning and mixing, developed into avant-garde architectural arguments. The modernist zoning practice and its implementation in contemporary cities has extended well into the 21st century. The metropolitan footprint of all major cities is outstripped by a vast, global, peri-urban hinterland that provides the power, water, waste disposal, carbon sequestration, consumer goods, and food that cities require to exist. The peri-urbanism of production and the urbanism of consumption have become parallel domains that operate concurrently, but separately, rarely coming into contact. This disconnect is exacerbated through architecture and the design disciplines, which rarely engage with the peri-urban sites of production, and for whom the question of density in cities has become a lifestyle marketing challenge.

The need to densify cities has never been more urgent. The world sits at the precipice of a global catastrophe, with the dual challenges of accelerating climate change driven by human-caused greenhouse gas emissions and biodiversity collapse, overshadowing all other issues. According to the United Nations,[2] the world has until 2030 to prevent irreversible damage to the world's climate and environmental systems, with others claiming that threshold has already been crossed.[3] Cities are responsible for as much as 70 percent of the world's greenhouse gas emissions,[4] a figure that includes the construction of cities; energy to maintain them; and waste disposal, transport, and consumables to support urban populations. While technological innovation, such as the emergence of sustainable power sources and electrifying everything have the potential to dramatically reduce the carbon footprint of cities, this process is slow, dependent on massive capital investment, and largely sits beyond the control of designers. While we can take measures to design buildings that are more efficient, we largely rely on macroeconomic and political levers in the final environmental impact of design. The largest single impact that architects and urban designers can make to the climate crisis is the tightening of our cities. The carbon footprint of a city is inextricably linked to its scale. Reducing the physical footprint of a city is the most obvious and direct way to reduce its environmental footprint—for both carbon emissions and ecological impact.

While this sounds simple, the imperative to reduce global urban footprints has coincided with the

1.1 Housing in London

c1870s.

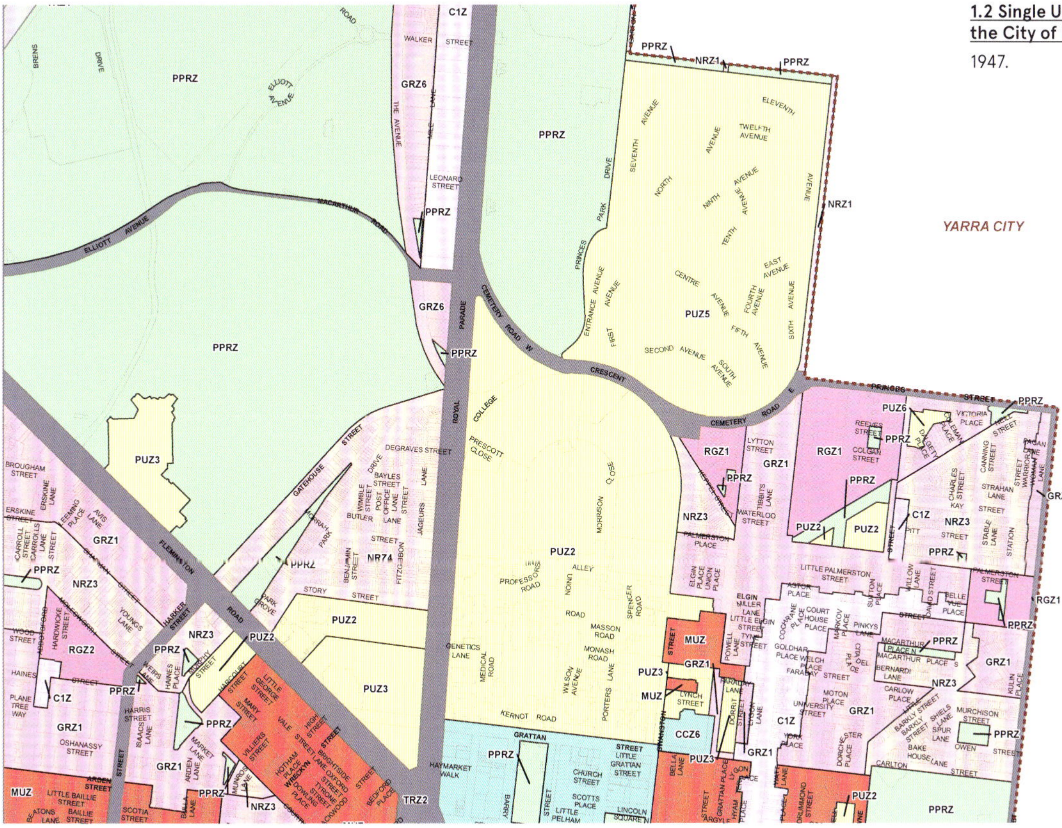

1.2 Single Use Zoning in the City of Melbourne

1947.

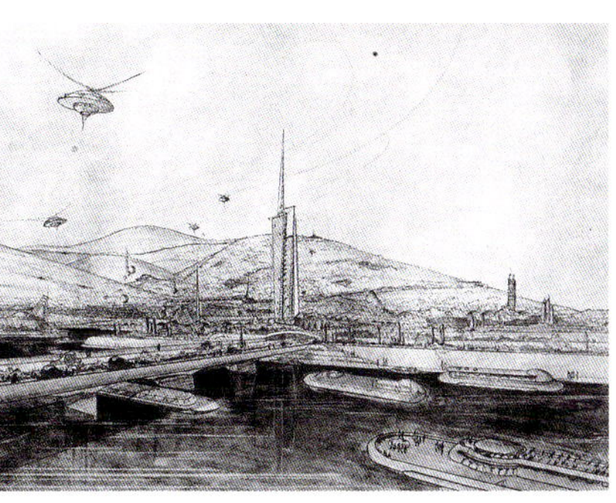

1.3 Broadacre City Frank Lloyd Wright

1934.

1.4 Delhi

By some estimates Delhi will be the largest city in the world by 2050 with an urban population of almost 50 million.

explosion of the urban population. It is well-quoted that in the 21st century, for the first time in human history, more people are living inside cities than outside of them. The global population, currently 8 billion, will continue to rise throughout the 21st century, with an expected global population of 9.7 billion by 2050.[5] Of this population, around 68 percent will live in cities. This means that over the next 30 years, globally, around 2.47 billion people[6] will be born or move into cities. Most of this growth will take place within the Global South, through the rapid urbanisation of megacities in Asia and Africa. The challenge for architects and urbanists therefore becomes the development of design models that allow for the compression of urban environments, while absorbing an expanding population within a model of density that is not only efficient but also desirable, and socially and economically sustainable.

Discussions of urban density cannot be separated from discussions of production urbanism. As noted, in the history of cities, the segregation of production spaces from consumption spaces is a very recent phenomenon. In recent decades, particularly after Jane Jacob's criticism of modern city planning and zoning divisions in the 1960s and Christopher Alexander's call for urban diversity and the inclusion of ordinary elements of daily life in design and urban policy in the 1970s,[7] the notion of dense cities as social and economic entities where living and working co-exist has resurfaced. Attention to production in metropolitan cities has dramatically increased over the last decade. The improvement and applicability of technologies such as artificial intelligence and robotics and the recent experience of the COVID-19 disease pandemic have shown that living and working can co-exist. For instance, according to the Australian Institute of Family Studies, in June 2021, two-thirds of Australians were working from home,[8] transforming the mono-functional site of a house into a mixed-use space. Manufacturing has also changed, both in terms of the way in it is conducted, with smart technologies that produce less waste and fewer emissions, but also in the way that products are procured and distributed. The technology revolution of the 2000s, developing platforms such as Taobao, has shifted global production away from large-scale mass production, towards a highly distributed model of small-scale, on-demand manufacturing.

Over the last few years, speculative and actual design models for bringing production back into cities have become a significant trend in the education and practice of architecture and urban design. Several research centres and platforms, such as the Fab City, the City of Making, and Architecture Workroom Brussels are already working on these models. Scholarly outputs such as Production Urbanism: The Meta Industrial City (2021) and New Industrial Urbanism: Designing Places for Production (2022) are examples of recent efforts to explore solutions to bringing production back to cities.[9]

What many of these investigations overlook, however, is the coupling of density with production. It is not enough to return production spaces to cities, only for them to sprawl endlessly. Likewise, we cannot design compact cities and simply ignore the global hinterland that supports them. We must densify our cities, tightening not only the spaces of consumption and living, but also closely coupling and integrating the productive spaces that support our cities. House, Precinct, Territory: Design Strategies for the Productive City explores the consolidation of production spaces as a hypothetical scenario for three cities, using detailed design responses as a methodology for teasing out the challenges, but also the opportunities, inherent in this approach.

At a high level, the folding of productive spaces into dense urban environments suggests benefits of reducing the physical footprint of production facilities and embodied and ongoing energy requirements, and also a dramatic reduction in transport and logistics emissions. In addition, compact cities are of greater social benefit to their residents. Compact cities contribute to residents' wellbeing by enhancing walkability and creating resilient communities in which informal exchange at the interpersonal level and the transmission of tacit knowledge can occur owing to the proximity of sites of production and consumption.

In the post-global period, where cities rely on vast international supply chains to provide food, consumer goods, energy, and waste disposal, the tight integration of a city with its productive hinterland provides a framework for greater security and sovereignty. However, recent world events, such as COVID-19 in 2020, the closure of the Suez Canal in 2021, and the Russian invasion of Ukraine in 2022, have disrupted global manufacturing, shipping, energy, and food distribution with catastrophic consequences for urban populations. The dysfunctionality of current city planning approaches at times of crisis has become more conspicuous. While there are obvious geographic resource limitations, producing food, energy, and goods, and disposing of their by-products as much as possible within the jurisdiction that they are consumed, is a way to manage the efficient operation of the city. It is now an appropriate time to reconsider urban planning approaches and develop design models for cities that integrate production and consumption, understanding the inherent potential of these models in times of future natural or human induced crises.

Bringing production into the space of consumption provides a framework for oversight and governance. Goods can be produced, consumed, and disposed of within the same legal and regulatory framework. This strategy would have implications for consumer protection and industrial relations. While emerging technologies, such as blockchain networks, have suggested methods for ensuring security and quality in extended supply chains, there is no substitute for being able to experience the production of the thing you will ultimately consume. Likewise, production within the same jurisdiction as consumption has the potential for winding back the more opportunistic and egregious aspects of globalised capitalism. A productive city is one in which it is not possible to simply move production to a different jurisdiction to reduce labour costs. Production and consumption occur within the same workplace law and economic context. To facilitate the mixing of land uses, a reform of the existing zoning codes within our contemporary cities seems cogent.

It is unlikely that our cities can be swiftly returned to being productive in the way they once were; however, this book explores the potential for the iterative and progressive retro-fitting of cities towards an

1.5 The *Ever Given* disaster in 2021 revealed the fragility of global shipping networks.

1.6 The production of power, capture of water, manufacturing of goods, cultivation of food and treatment of waste have been removed from cities.

incrementally greater percentage of production within their footprint. Within this scenario, the densification and retrofitting of cities through the architecture of addition seems a valid pathway to consider. The idea of additive transformation has already attracted architects and urban designers such as Chilean architect and scholar Rodrigo Perez de Arce, who, in 1980, regarded this approach as "a balanced form of development" and an appropriate replacement for growth with extension and substitution. Perez de Arce's proposal was later expanded and tested by practitioners and developers such as British architect Roger Zogolovitch, who recognised the need to reorder the city's land use structure. Zogolovitch called for an urban transformation by infilling the city's empty sites, or what he called the gap sites.[10] The iterative adaptation of our cities to become more dense and more productive could be a pathway to produce a model of urbanism that is more sustainable and more equitable.

This book explores possible future visions for the retrofitting of urban environments to become more efficient through a reciprocity between production, consumption, and living. The medium of this research is in architectural design, tested through highly particular and specific circumstances with the ambition of providing the reader with design strategies transferable to varied contexts. The intention of this publication is to explore the implications of high-density production urbanism at a series of scales—domestic (house), urban (precinct), and regional (territory)—in three locations—respectively Brisbane, Seoul, and

Melbourne—proposing design models for future urban environments remade for greater resilience.

It is this approach that has determined the structure of the book. The `Scenario-Based Modelling' section focuses on the methodology and explains the common methods adopted to conduct the research. The central section of the book is divided into three parts, dedicated to the analysis of urban production at the small (domestic/house), medium (precinct), and large (territorial) scale. This approach seeks to usefully look at the same problem (the productive city) from different standpoints and varied levels of urban grain and scale. We have applied these scale categories to three cities of metropolitan size (Brisbane, Seoul, and Melbourne), which are fast growing urban centres in the Asia-Pacific Region. They are all urban centres of large areas with a global drive, belong to similar commercial circuits, and operate in comparable cultural environments. Each part includes a dialogue with external scholars as interlocutor, chosen to bring complementary critical input and provocations on the productive scenarios put forward by the authors. Each dialogue is the result of a forum organised in the form of an extended conversation, which was recorded and transcribed. The book ends with—Urban Production Futures—that reflects on the findings of each part and puts forward a discussion on the design strategies proposed, while also considering what has been learnt in setting forth ideas for increasing productivity in contemporary cities.

1.7 The suburbs of Brisbane are adapted to become productive.

Endnotes

1. Churchman, A. "Disentangling the Concept of Density." Journal of Planning Literature 13, No. 4 (May 1999), 392.
2. https://press.un.org/en/2019/ga12131.doc.htm.
3. https://www.science.org/doi/10.1126/science.abn7950#core-collateral-purchase-access.
4. https://blogs.worldbank.org/sustainablecities/cutting-global-carbon-emissions-where-do-cities-stand#:~:text=Cities%20account%20for%20over%2070,constructed%20with%20carbon%2Dintensive%20materials.
5. https://www.un.org/development/desa/pd/sites/www.un.org.development.desa.pd/files/wpp2022_summary_of_results.pdf.
6. https://unhabitat.org/sites/default/files/2022/06/wcr_2022.pdf.
7. See Jacobs, Jane. The Death and Life of Great American Cities. New York: Random House, 1961, and Alexander, Christopher, Sara Ishikawa, and Murray Silverstein. A Pattern Language: Towns, Buildings, Construction. Oxford: Oxford University Press, 1977.
8. Baxter, Jennifer, Diana Warren. "Two thirds of Australians are working from home." Australian Institute of Family Studies (June 2021). https://aifs.gov.au/media/two-thirds-australians-are-working-home#:~:text=The%20Families%20in%20Australia%20Survey,to%2042%25%20pre%2DCOVID.
9. See Yim, Dongwoo and Rafael Luna (editors). Production Urbanism: The Meta Industrial City. New York: Welly, 2021, and Ben-Joseph, Eran and Tali Hatuka. New Industrial Urbanism: Designing Places for Production. New York and Abingdon: Routledge, 2022.
10. See Perez de Arce, Rodrigo. Urban Transformations and the Architecture of Additions. Abingdon: Routledge, 2014, and Zogolovitch, Roger. Shouldn't We All Be Developers? London: Artifice Books on Architecture, 2015).

SCENARIO-BASED MODELLING FOR URBAN DESIGN

The common method used in the development of the three projects included in this book—house, precinct, and territory—can be described as scenario-based modelling, although this is heavily tempered by close observation of each city, following techniques of everyday urbanism, as well as by spatial modelling.[1] As such, the design approach seeks a balanced dialogue between futurology, a technique relying on evidence-based speculations, and the identification of latent capacities in existing conditions.

Scenario-based modelling can be defined as a rich and detailed portrait of a plausible future world, one sufficiently vivid that a planner can clearly see and comprehend the problems, challenges, and opportunities that such an environment would present. A scenario in this context is not intended as a prediction of the future, rather a plausible framing of what the city may become—one of a series of possible futures. Scenarios are narratives built through carefully constructed plots, rooted in the reality of current trends and events.[2] They do not directly map the future but can assist with its planning, by making people aware of uncertainties and stimulating the imagination towards initiating learning processes.

Rational and structured through evidenced-based readings and analysis, scenarios are one of the most popular and persuasive methods used in futurology, the systematic forecasting of the future based on evidencing current tendencies in society. Government planners, corporate strategists, and military analysts use scenarios to aid decision making. The term *scenario* was first introduced into planning and decision making by Herman Kahn in connection with military and strategic studies undertaken by RAND in the 1950s.[3] Among the key strengths of a scenario process is the ability to influence and reshape ways of thinking. A fixed mindset in which the focus placed on one forecast future is forgone, replaced by thinking that opens towards a number of possible alternative futures. Rather than simple formal solutions, scenarios point to how circumstances might interrelate by careful forward looking. This process of design thinking produces a postulated development of events—not a forecast—prompting guided speculations on possible pathways. This research adopts the scenario as its central premise, grounded by the belief that the city already enacts the potential of its development through the existence of urban traces. As understood through this research, the role of the designer is to identify those traces and chart their trajectories as a creative act of design generation. The research outcomes are determinedly open-ended and consciously provisional—capable of alternative alignments—ones that embrace the productive uncertainties that emerge in the continuous evolving of urban environments. While the application of scenario-based methods has been considered in relation to landscape and environmental planning,[4] in this book we explicitly bring scenario-based thinking to a modelling approach for urban design.

In charting scenarios through the House, Precinct, and Territory projects, several characteristics of our urban design method can be noted. These include the use of observation-based analysis, the making of speculative amplifications, designing from data, the practice of retrofitting, and the deployment of exhibiting as critique.

Observation-Based on Analysis of Specific Found Conditions

Each of the three projects emerged from observations of particular and immediate urban conditions that are already in existence. They are expansions of a productive capacity unfolding as grassroots phenomena in the city. Observational analysis leads to the orchestration of particular scenarios where the nascent urban production is radically expanded and proposed as a dominant model through a retrofit to a piece of the city.

In the house project, the productive capacity of the suburban residential environment in West End, Brisbane, Australia is observed from living amongst it, and from monitoring the amplification and diversification of the use of the house during the 2020 COVID-19 disease pandemic. Single dwellings with micro-interventions of enterprise are already scattered through the city's inner suburbs. These single dwellings are leveraging the significant, but open and loose space of individual properties in a low-density domestic context, freeing the underexploited potential for productive activities that have nonetheless existed, or been latent at small scale for some time.

In the precinct project, the observation of the immediate and existing conditions of the city in Seongsu, a workshop precinct of Seoul, Korea, involves a close reading of the surface of buildings and the productive elements attached to them. The scenario here envisages the systematic use of such elements and their full integration in the aesthetic of the city, while consciously embracing

2.1 Micro-enterprise operating from a typical Queenslander style house in Brisbane.

2.2 Seongsu in Seoul has been modified through innumerbale "accessories" that adapt the city for production.

their capacity to enhance production. In the careful and detailed drawing of the city as found and operating now, the distinction between urban planning structures, architectural design, and the accreted additions to the built fabric are entirely dissolved. At the same time, and by implication, the distinction between the productive spaces and the inhabited spaces of the city are also fully dissolved. As such, working, production, and living are seen to co-habit in a new dynamic.

In the territory project, the scenario of agricultural production within greater Melbourne, Australia, emerges from the significant areas of semi-rural land falling within a large urban growth boundary that already predicts future housing expansion and the loss of productive capacity in the land. The definition of the growth boundary, designed to curb the sprawl of the city, codifies the peri-urban development superseding rural territory. The observations identify areas that are already agricultural in character, post-industrial zones with underutilised productive capacity, as well as observing redundancies that exist, even within the dense high-rise core of the central business district. The scenario also follows the endurance of vast areas of agricultural land surrounding the city that have been subject to environmental degradation. The method used in this project is to quantify capacity for agricultural production within the urban plan. This opportunity is identified at the scale of the single plot of land yet is able to be extended to the urban form more generally. That extension is necessary given the vast areas required for food production to feed the city.

Forming Design from Speculative Amplifications

If we differentiate the *tactical* from the *strategic* (as Michel de Certeau does), then this research is premised on observing those tactical uses of spaces, now operative, which misalign with systems and norms, and the strategic frameworks of urban governance.[5] The new design proposals created are specifically related to ways in which spaces are currently appropriated within the city. Such tactical appropriations are, however, greatly expanded—notional amplifications of the urban conditions in which they are seen. This work of expanding on tactics, undertaken through design, elevates the tactical into new strategic urban opportunities—ones that are provocative and open-ended rather than codified and fixed. Even at the territorial scale, which may appear more overtly strategic in method, the project begins with the proposition of converting single buildings to agricultural production. Tactics emerge as an adaptation to, or a repurposing of, the regulated built and urban environment as it is. At times, that adaptation might be described as a deliberate misuse. In methodological terms, the conversion of an urban tactic into a newly formed strategy demands the suspension of some of the current assumptions about how the city is controlled, attending instead to what can emerge despite those controls. It may even be that, when expanded, these tactics require almost no transgression of codified controls, but may transgress market or cultural norms. The process does involve taking a situation that might be an exception or an aberration (even if permissible) and expanding it to the norm. It is qualitatively different to observe the occasional market garden in a city, to observing a city where one finds their groceries produced in their own neighbourhood or in one nearby. It is also qualitatively different for a resident selling goods intermittently from the streetside adjacent to their house, to a scenario where a street is reshaped and all the houses are co-opted for small enterprises and the production and exchange of goods. A particular precinct of Seoul might offer a ready-made model for a productive city by observing various pieces of functional machinery applied to façades, but if that model is expanded and proposed as the loose template for a whole megacity, then the qualitative impact is entirely different.

2.3 The suburbs of Melbourne are defined by an excess of space, and the capacity for productive infill.

2.4 The cataloguing of production accessories in Seongsu suggests the potential for these components to be applied to the city at scale.

Designing as Physical Modelling From Data

In each of the projects, the overall strategy advanced by the design emerges from an evidence base that describes a particular condition of the city. Because there is not a singular method of collection, approaches vary. For example, in the house project in Brisbane, evidence is gathered through observational studies based in techniques of ethnographic research; in this case, the social encounter of individuals making or exchanging goods and services on the public edges of private spaces. Such activities in the city were witnessed and recorded and then captured at a measured scale in architectural views for comparison and analysis. In the precinct project in Seoul, evidence is gathered via a scenographic approach. Drawn scenes from observations of places in the precinct revealed a set of accessories or accoutrements to buildings that are otherwise excluded from consideration as part of the conscious act of architecture and design. A visual record of the urban ensemble in its entirety thus revealed the accretion of elements and built information layered onto what is understood as the conventionally built, designed, or approved form of the precinct.

The body of evidence might also be expressed as data only—as numbers or quantities or even infographics. A scenario might be expressed or quantified as a set of measurable, but abstract, conditions. The design process here is understood as modelling akin to economic modelling. That is, testing a scenario and working through the consequences of a set of data. What does it look like if houses in Brisbane become sites for microenterprise and exchange? What does it look like if the accretions necessary to create opportunities for self-sufficiency within a productive precinct in Seoul are deliberately acknowledged, accounted for, and celebrated? What does it look like if repurposed or reclaimed sites in Melbourne grow all the food required for the city? In the research, the modelling of scenarios from the data is a critical move, one central to the methodology. Giving spatial form to data lays out the consequences of a scenario, realised as an urban phenomenon. There is no intent to claim an inevitable form to the scenario, rather the aim is to register the possible consequences that can accrue. The qualitative data from the modelling is inseparable from the quantifiable numbers associated with the scenario. Spatialising the proposition provides a grasp on a scenario, allowing its urban affects to be interrogated.

The Practice of Retrofitting and Acknowledging the Form of the City

The form and spatial consequences of a scenario matter. They are critical to understanding that scenario, both in the sense of its projective qualities and in its impact, which relates to the city as an action of retrofitting. This approach is built on the understanding that the future transformation of the city emerges from the city as it exists and traits of transformation have already taken form through spatial evolution and accretion in the urban environment. The obvious question of any scenario, "What does it look like?" is to be taken seriously. Typically, the treatment of urban design scenarios

2.5 Physical model of a high-density agricultural production facility in the centre of Melbourne.

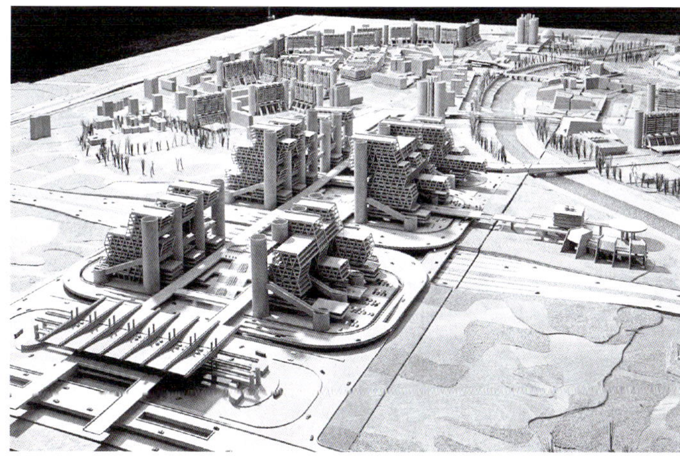

2.6 Large-scale future visions have often relied on a tabula rasa starting point.

2.7 The scenarios explored draw upon a process of adaptation and adjustment of the existing urban fabric at different scales.

bifurcates into future-oriented approaches that treat the city as a redundant tabula rasa for complete rethinking or is based on a preservation impulse that seeks to halt the processes of replacement. The former position has dominated modernity, while the latter is set as a reaction to modernism's strategy of erasure. A radical retrofitting method must account for both the preservation of the evolved city—as a site for effective re-use and a re-imagining of that space into something entirely new. Giving form by deploying a practice of retrofitting is critical to demonstrating the viability of a scenario, just as it is critical to testing its acceptance and uptake. The method allows and demands iterations of varied versions of the model, and of testing various refinements of its form.

Modelling and Exhibiting as Reflection and Critique

The modelling process is neither linear nor purely illustrative for any given scenario. Rather, the urban scenario is developed through and with the production of drawings and physical models that inform the parameters of a scenario. Further, the act of physically modelling, exhibiting, reflecting, and re-iterating the propositions is critical to the refinement and adaptation of scenarios. Casting the three projects at different scales was also crucial. The house, precinct, and territory parameters were set to the nature of the investigation—their scale reflected that of the observations and took a key role in scenario building. At the same time, each of the three projects were addressing comparable questions at different scales, and the reflection on each in parallel clarified a developed position toward the productive city. The dialogue between Brisbane, Seoul, and Melbourne as the loci of the three projects grew from the particular and specific observations of each design project, but also generated comparison both at scale and location for the projects. The questions of applicability and of repeatability of each of the scenarios to the other locations remains a live question.

A first stage of the works for the three projects was exhibited as physical models and drawings to a public audience and accompanied by a round table discussion in an exhibition space. A second tranche of design work followed, which reframed and developed the proposition, and was then re-exhibited in a different public location, with a subsequent round of reflective discussions. This process was not simply a mode of disseminating the work, but is a part of its methodology. This approach is probably self-evident to any designer, but it is counter to a method that sets a rule or policy and then imagines the design work as an illustration of that rule. In this case, the method reflects the iterative and accretive nature of the urban scenarios. The scenario is not a final outcome but a work that is always provisional—capable of recasting by cycles of conjecture and critique undertaken through public presentation and back through the research.

Critical to the understanding of the scenarios advanced in these projects is the role of the spatial modelling of both the future and existing city.

It is equally critical to understand the spatial modelling as a series of counterfactual possibilities—making narratives of alternative and unexpected trajectories. Neither forecasts nor prescriptions, the scenarios are descriptions of possibility already latent, and already viable action.[6]

2.8 Spatial and formal propositions were developed, exhibited, reflected on and then further developed as a mode of research.

2.9 Preliminary design proposal for a site in Brisbane exhibited at the Making Tight Exhibition in Melbourne.

Endnotes

1. Chase, John Leighton, Margaret Crawford, and John Kaliski (editors.) Everyday urbanism. New York: Monacelli Press, 2008.
2. Smith, Frank, Aim Sinpeng, Ralph Holz, Sarah Logan, Jonathon Hutchinson, and Hui Xue. "Scenario Analysis." Australia's Cybersecurity Future(s): It's January 2024. Does Australia Still Have the Internet? Australian Strategic Policy Institute, 2018. http://www.jstor.org/stable/resrep23056.4.
3. Founded in 1948 in the United States after World War II to connect military planning with research and development decisions, RAND is a research-based organisation that develops solutions to public policy challenges to improve policy and decision making through research and analysis.
4. Shearer, Allan, W. "Approaching scenario-based studies: three perceptions about the future and considerations for landscape planning." Environment and Planning B: Planning and Design (Vol. 32, 2005) 67–87.
5. See de Certeau, Michel. The Practice of Everyday Life. Berkeley: University of California Press, 1988.
6. Beautiful Trouble. "The tactics of everyday life." https://beautifultrouble.org/toolbox/tool/the-tactics-of-everyday-life/.

1
HOUSE

(Brisbane)

Silvia Micheli
Antony Moulis
Peyman Akhgar

Domestic Production in the City

Is it possible for our cities to intensify their productive capacity by developing scenarios where living and working co-exist? Strengthening the residential property as a space of production can start from the redesign of its boundary edge. Applied at scale to the city, the repurposed boundary can unleash potential for interactive, vibrant neighbourhoods open to the agency of individuals.

Some 89% of Australia's population now lives in cities, where residential space dominates urban development.[1] Increased demand for residential growth keeps consuming industrial and agricultural lands, pushing productive areas further outside the city. As urban agglomeration continues its inexorable advance in the Australian suburbs, this issue can also be recognised at a global level. The 2020 European Union New Leipzig Charter on city transformation points to the opportunity to develop sustainable green city initiatives in tandem with the drive to more productive cities—an idea with broad implications.[2] This call challenges the conventional logic of land-use policies and zoning, which favour urban space allocation to residential, office, commercial, or leisure functions, effectively leaving out productive space from cities.

However, activities of production are taking place in residential spaces, often with minimal acknowledgement, scant visibility, and a lack of appropriate infrastructure to support work practices. Since early 2020, individuals have adapted to the demands of working from home, shifting the sites

3.1 Timber fence of a detached house in West End, Brisbane.

of productivity in the city, as well as working behaviours. The COVID-19 disease and the resulting pandemic, with its lockdowns and limits on mobility, accelerated the use of residential space for production, affecting the way people work at a mass scale. What is the consequence of this significant shift, and what does this mean for productivity and the economic redesign of cities in the long term? Recognising the detached suburban house as a prime location for urban production, our project embraces the dimension of the microscale to advance residential typologies through design, combining innovative domestic working arrangements with economic models evolving in neighbourhoods. Developing design strategies to support new, localised, suburban businesses can lead to revitalised communities, less commuting (lower carbon footprint), and better quality of life for increased wellbeing.

It is recognised that the productive model deriving from the phenomenon of working from home, which picked up in usage during the pandemic, created knock-on effects. Among these effects was a rise in feelings of social isolation and related health issues,[3] as well as the urban effect of emptying out central business districts and traditional work and retail spaces.[4] However, many of these outcomes relate to office-centred working models, whereas our project embraces the notion of production in its widest dimension, including manufacturing and production of artisanal goods and their exchange and sale—activities that seed the relaunching of localised economies and communities. Also, our analysis and design proposition are not limited to workspaces within private properties. Instead, we concentrate on liminal spaces and how they can be activated to increase networks of exchange within the neighbourhood context [3.1].

Dormant Edge

A walk around the residential suburbs of Brisbane quickly uncovers kilometres of fencing lines. All different, and yet all the same, the succession of individual fences reflects the insularity of the private properties they frame, with their palings, grass verges, gates, railings, letterboxes, garden beds, plants, and trees. The materiality of the fence line comes into play through uses of timber, brick, metal, and chain wire; or simply constructed landscaping. Different levels of division are offered, from visual segregation to shades of porosity and stark openness. The function of the fences is twofold: on one hand, they perform a traditional ornamental role, mainly through their construction, shape, and planting; on the other hand, they provide privacy and security, regulating access to the domestic site from the public domain. Limited to these functional roles, the property boundary edge reflects the concept of the suburban dormitory in its quiet and monofunctional character [3.2]. The presence of the fence is discrete and almost overlooked. Strung along the streetscape, their edge types and planting schemes reveal a conventional seriality. In the long, visual, urban perspectives of the streets, they appear with remarkable consistency, variations on an endless theme, making up the socially agreed division between public and private life. One after the other, the different fences tend to merge. Considered in their sequence, collapsing one into another, they form long ribbons that hem in residential blocks [3.3].

Understanding the collective nature of the fencing system in the suburbs, not necessarily as the ultimate limit of the private property but rather as a dominant urban element, we put forward the notion of the *dormant edge*. This is an edge characterised by its prolonged inactivity—apparently empty of all use but the most symbolic presentation of the house outwardly, the framing of its presence, its ultimate decorative and protective threshold. Ubiquitous, characterless, at times seemingly useless if not for its symbolic nature, the dormant edge can now be seen as an opportunity for new design investigation and intervention. Through the lens of the dormant edge, we recognise the substantial amount of underutilised urban infrastructure that the contemporary suburban city (un)consciously encompasses. With its conspicuous low-density sprawl, Brisbane is striking for the amount of fencing system that distinguishes its urban image, becoming a conducive case study.

Brisbane reflects common urban strategies present in cities developed from the 19th century into the 20th century, which were patterned on gridded planning arrangements, only to conform over time to the zoned

3.2 A residential house with dormant fence line.

Residential sites comprise almost 80% of Brisbane suburbs. These sites are mostly defined by dormant edges.

3.3 Dormant edges in West End, Brisbane.

The dormant edges of Brisbane represent an opportunity for rethinking the relationship between the public domain and private properties.

3.4 Axonometric map of a Brisbane suburb charactrized with dormant fence lines.

Brisbane suburbs are made of thousands of metres of dormant fence line along residential sites.

city paradigm (dwelling, recreation, work, and transportation). The rational and organisational logic of Functionalism operates on a quasi-scientific urban approach. It develops spatial divisions that ratify the segregation of human activities, prioritising transportation and movement between zones justified by concepts of efficiency and health in urban circulation. Seen from an economic perspective, the designated place of living (typically the house within the suburb) acts as a site of consumption, separate of sites of commercial production operating in zones elsewhere and connected through vast distribution chains. Within the current economic/planning paradigm, zones for industry and shopping constitute key nodes in a network of commerce with the suburban house, singular and atomised, as its endpoint serviced by the movement of residents collecting goods or the arrival of internet purchased items.

This order of segregation in urban space affects the character and structure of the domestic block in relation to the street. However, current regulatory frameworks mandate strict divisions between zones for residential, commercial, and industrial activities. The regulation that requires road setbacks at the front of domestic sites has made the existence of any form of built intervention along these major residential edges unfeasible, reducing fences to almost bidimensional components.[5] Such a mandate does not allow for multi-use spaces at the front of residential sites along what we describe as the dormant edges in suburban Brisbane.

Taken individually, the fences reflect the width of the residential blocks they define, oscillating between an average of ten to twenty metre frontages. However, by summing them up, their length becomes somehow impressive [3.4]. For instance, in three densely populated inner-city suburbs of Brisbane (West End, Paddington, and Annerley), located only a few kilometres away from Brisbane's central business district, the length of residential edges respectively tallies at 25,000 metres, 41,000 metres, and 52,000 metres. These numbers disclose the latent potential hidden in those lineal surfaces to enable future use as productive spaces where material exchange and social interaction can occur. With a population set to increase from 2.2 million to 4.2 million by 2050,[6] Brisbane's suburban fencing system can offer an opportunity to rethink the way neighbourhoods are organised and used and re-evaluate the relationship between public and private space.

Activated Edge

Intensifying the nature of the suburban street edge as an interface between the private property and the community, the dormant edge can awaken to become what we term the *activated edge*—an operative stage for localised economies upon which other uses are engaged and released. In recent years, instigated by the lockdown due to COVID-19, Brisbane residents increasingly seeded their own uses of such edges as an organic and bottom-up reaction to the restrictions, seemingly at odds with suburban convention and imposed regulations. New habits emerged as domestic front yards and their fence lines transformed into spaces of productive exchange and display, turning the monofunctional site of the house into a multifunctional space. As a result, the house and its ancillary spaces have progressively moved from being sites of consumption to ones of microscale production, now re-considered through strategies of highly localised activation.

Times of economic recession and urban emergencies can prove catalytic for altering the established modes according to which the city is conceived and used, as local populations adapt to new conditions. COVID-19, which forced most people in Brisbane within a five-kilometre radius of their homes, provoked a surge in home-based businesses within residential sites to preserve and manage productivity—a phenomenon that is still evolving.[7] The concurrence of living and working—that is consuming and producing—on sites that are zoned as residential[8] has triggered a process of transformation with profound implications for the urban environments they are nestled in. While individuals were confined to their private property, the fence was progressively appreciated as a buffer between private and public life—an urban divider as well as a connector. Repurposed in response to changing circumstances, these spaces questioned and challenged the ubiquitous zoning laws and explicit functional divisions that structurally underlie the residential suburb pattern across Brisbane.

The co-existence of production and consumption in residential areas is a feature of the urban history of Brisbane, whose residential suburbs used to be serviced by so-called corner stores (local general stores). These small retail facilities operated as commercial spaces fronting the street edge, usually attached at the rear or side to a residence. However, in the 1980s, with the approval of Sunday trading for larger grocery stores and supermarkets, traditional corner stores progressively lost their profitability in local trading as larger chain stores located in car-accessed shopping centres took greater commercial command.[9] The most recent revived interest in localised forms of production aligns with the implications of the progressive emergence of

21st century practices, such as circular economies and zero carbon footprint strategies, where economic value is found through practices of integration and hybridity in mixed-use neighbourhoods.[10]

Drawing on an observational approach known as everyday urbanism, a close examination of the everyday life of people residing in Brisbane's inner-city suburban neighbourhoods revealed an increased tendency in the use of liminal spaces in private properties [3.5]. Introduced by Margaret Crawford, John Chase, and John Kaliski in 1999, everyday urbanism is an approach to the city that looks at routines and uncoded situations of everyday life, seeking "to release the powers of creativity and imagination already present within daily life as the means of transforming urban experience and the city".[11] Everyday urbanism built on late 20th century theories to oppose the artificial and highly regulated urban schemes introduced by modern design and planning.[12] We share the view that the city, beyond its built forms, is also "a social product, created out of the demands of everyday use and the social struggles of urban inhabitants".[13] By acknowledging the dimension of the everyday which reveals "a fabric of space and time defined by a complex realm of social practices"[14], we observe and document real social phenomena through ethnographic studies, extrapolating their design potential. This bottom-up approach has informed the conceptual framing of the dormant edge and the activated edge, evidenced in the Brisbane suburban context.

The mapping of small-scale interventions that have occurred in Brisbane since the pandemic, and even before it, demonstrates the widespread nature of niche businesses across the city. Taking place in residential zones, fully regulated as such, the spontaneous activation of edges shows how production

3.5 Street vendor, West End, Brisbane.
Arranged on a public footpath, this street vendor is selling second-hand books and clothes, turning the previously dormant edge into an active interstitial space.

3.6 Street plant nursery and shop, West End, Brisbane.

Located on a shady footpath, the nursery is set against the fence line. An under-croft car park and sideyard are repurposed as spaces to grow and prepare plants for sale.

exists at different scales and levels of occupation, on and within properties, and along fences connecting public and private spaces. The fence line, the private parking space, the house undercroft, and the backyard and sideyard are observed as sites of production and exchange, redefining the identity of what was traditionally considered the private property. Taking advantage of the ambiguity intrinsic to the edge—its dual private and public nature—we observe new activities and behaviours that activate the property in spontaneus entrepreneurial modes.

For example, a mango tree, whose medium crown has a thick foliage, covers a plastic table arranged with propagated plants. Located on the footpath in the shadow of the tree, the table is tightly set against the fence. While the selling side of the pop-up nursery interfaces directly with passers-by, on the private side, gardening tools are orderly located in the undercroft of the building, silently signalling a space of production (propagation workshop and storage). There is no evident sign of supervision, yet it feels like someone is looking down from one of the balconies, overseeing the enterprise. Within the highly localised chain of production, the undercroft and backyard function as the nursery space, where the resident grows plants, preparing them for sale [3.6]. The tables at the street edge house the shop—a space of commercial exchange where plants are displayed and accessible to the public, an exchange that is asynchronic. On another street, just outside the edge of a house, a bike servicing station has been installed for collective use [3.7 and 3.8]. The fence acts as the background for the bike service, which can be accessed by anyone at any time while passing along the street. The interaction of the bike servicing station with the footpath and the street is constantly negotiated with the community, reflecting local habits, and responding to changing needs. This station turns into a self-directing operation, a constant, mutual negotiation among people. A 24-hour bookstore, at the scale of a residential car space, is left unattended, with money to be placed in an honesty box. People are asked to pay either what they can, or what they want [3.9 and 3.10]. The examples abound, each reflecting individual agency and self-constructed modes [3.11 and 3.12; 3.13 and 3.14].

Performed as a result of a sudden necessity—and in so doing unveiling a high degree of resilience—these spontaneous productive activities embody a fundamental democratic process.[15] They play a vital role in strengthening the sense of place in both physical and spatial terms within a residential neighbourhood community. Multiple activated edges set in motion a shift in the use of the threshold between the public and the private, unveiling the city's potential to host more dynamic, vital, and mixed-used suburban spaces. That the house is repurposed through the agency of individuals speaks to London-based architect Roger Zogolovitch's idea that the urban context can be reinvented by means of the microscale, through independently motivated developments on small lots.[16]

3.7 and 3.8 Bike repair station, Dutton Park, Brisbane.

A bike servicing facility arranged for collective use. The interaction of the bike station with the footpath and the street is constantly negotiated with the community, reflecting local habits, and responding to changing needs.

<u>3.9 and 3.10 A local bookstore, Bardon, Brisbane.</u>

A 24-hour bookstore, at the scale of a car park, is left unattended, with money to be placed in an honesty box.

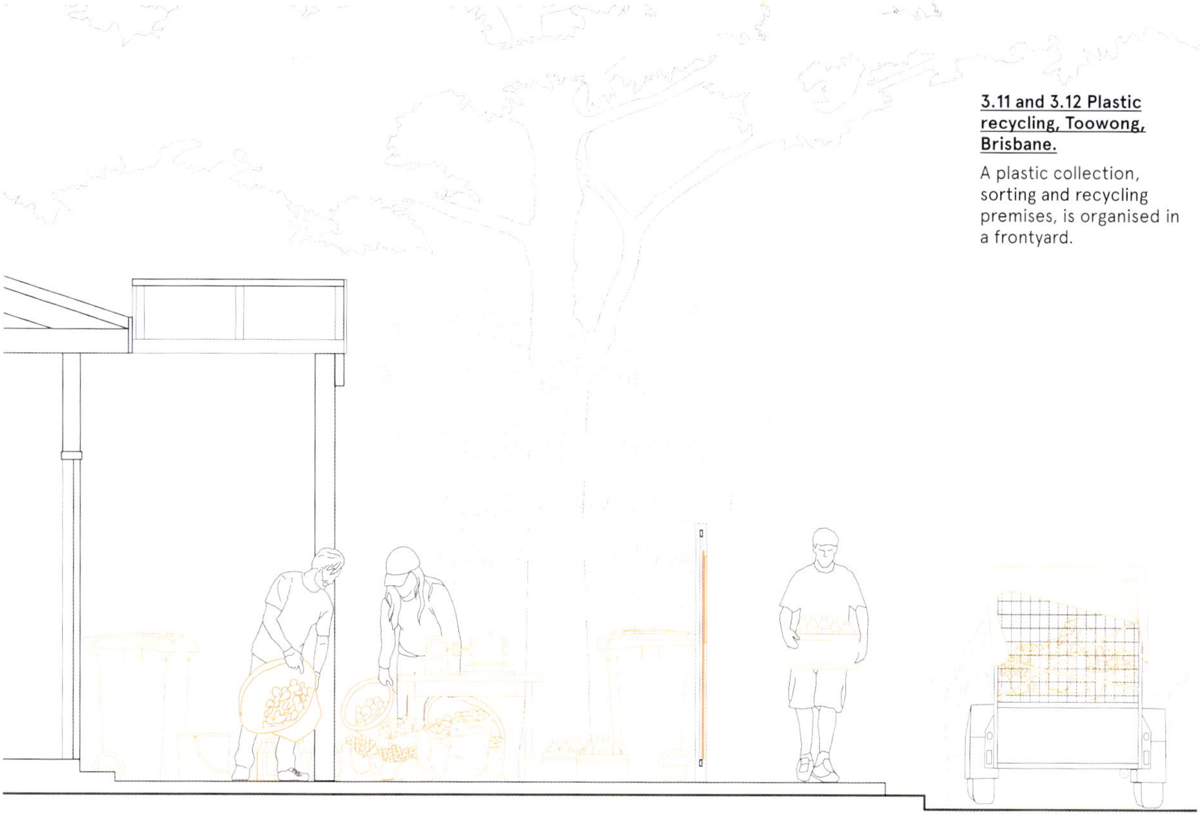

3.11 and 3.12 Plastic recycling, Toowong, Brisbane.

A plastic collection, sorting and recycling premises, is organised in a frontyard.

PLANTS FOR SALE
Community
Pantry
Take what you need.
Give if you can.

3.13 and 3.14 Fridge and plants for sale, Taringa, Brisbane.

A fridge and a small plant shop left unattended at the edge of a residential property, facilitating social interaction and item exchange in a suburban street.

Productive Edge

By rethinking one of its elements, namely the dormant edge, and releasing its latent design opportunity as a buffer between private and public spheres and the activated edge, the house can intensify its presence in the urban texture, hosting functions that have been progressively lost through large-scale industrialisation, commercial zoning, and global distribution. While still the site of access, the boundary has potential to engage with urban/communal spaces, enhancing the experience of regulated, yet essential, human contact. This conceptual subversion translates into what we have called the *productive edge*, a boundary conceived as spatial device that is placed between the house and the street to generate connections and new relationships. This interstitial space is independent from the house, yet it functions with it. It also encourages and facilitates exchange of goods without the contiguous presence of buyer and seller.

This regained space of the edge, functionally flexible and therefore temporal in nature, is ambiguous—a semi-public space of encounter for the re-negotiation of the domestic sphere with its public edges. During the pandemic, the space at the boundary became a safety buffer, providing a refuge from the street and, in the most extreme conditions, from the house itself. In, through, and after the pandemic, the edge has proved itself to be open, porous, and interactive. The need for flexibility demands the intervention of a new type, not of the house itself but in relation to it and complementing it. The productive edge emerges from the premise of a site within the site, a concept that begins with the appropriation of urban voids and terrain vague, ready to be claimed for a newly constituted program. The edge lies on the limit of existing built space and is not private nor public space per se, but fundamentally a relation of both. It is a productive edge where the counter-posed narratives of exterior and interior overlap and openings can be choreographed to construct varying levels of access and filtering.

The concept of the productive edge was tested through design by the integration of structures on the boundary of residential sites, related to other work spaces of their properties. For instance, relatively small additions like a bike repair workshop, a plant micro-nursery and a second-hand clothes shop attached to the fence can significantly contribute to the activation of dormant neighbourhoods and their residents' social and economic life [3.15 and 3.16]. In the domain of urban farming, the fence has already attracted some attention, with attempts to convert this surface into vertical systems for growing fruit and vegetables. If repeated, these interventions can turn the pedestrian walkway from a circulation corridor into a route that stages a set of local urban encounters. The street also loses its neutral state as a mere passage and becomes a part of the social space in which vehicular traffic slows while encouraging community interactions. The inner parts of the domestic site will no longer remain a space of consumption but rather an activated site in which production is variously taking place as an intrinsic part of daily life.

Adding structures to the existing urban fabric aligns with what Rodrigo Perez de Arce called the "architecture of addition".[17] By this concept, the built environment would grow or increase by "the gradual accumulation of additional layers or matter",[18] and the result would therefore sit contrary to the rapid suburban sprawl of recent years, which literally expands the city beyond its borders. According to Perez de Arce, additive transformation can enhance the qualities of the city in three ways. Firstly, by gradually incorporating parts into existing structures, additive transformation extends the likelihood of the new structure being used for a prolonged period. Secondly, additive transformation is a low-cost process, as it is based on the retention of what already exists. And thirdly, this process of transformation ensures a sense of continuity, and contributes to the neighbourhood's sense of place in historical time by turning the buildings into repositories of successive interventions, and, spatially, by reinforcing the notion of space creation as an incremental process.

3.15 Design strategies for a second-hand clothes shop and a bike repair workshop.
These facilities act as spatial devices. They are placed between the house and the street where socio-commercial exchange can occur.

3.16 Design strategy for a bike repair workshop located in a suburban street.

The bike repair workshop facilitates urban commerce and communal experience at micro-scale.

The interaction of public and private along the productive edge generates a new social and political landscape, in which individuals become drivers in creating new economic relationships. As Manuel Castells states, "we are currently contemplating the emergence of new social landscapes, in which individualised persons strive to cope with the responsibility of constructing their built environment and networks of communication on the basis of who they are and what they want".[19]

The spaces formed around the boundary edge can therefore be identified as shared [3.17]. Shaped and defined by people, these spaces are categorised, according to James Holston, as "spaces of insurgent citizenship", characterful and specific, in contrast to the more abstract spaces generated by modern urban planners.[20] These new urban tri-dimensional edges of quotidian qualities can be conceptually identified as the third space (neither home nor workplace) bearing "the possibility of new meanings, activated through social action and the social imagination".[21] The productive edge can exist at any scale, time, and level of occupation. While our proposition is tested in Brisbane, the concept of the productive edge is also transferable to other urban contexts where high levels of urban regulation currently exist.

3.17 Transforming a dormant suburb into a productive neighbourhood.

The productive edge, if applied at the scale of the city, can turn streets into vibrant urban places of social encounter.

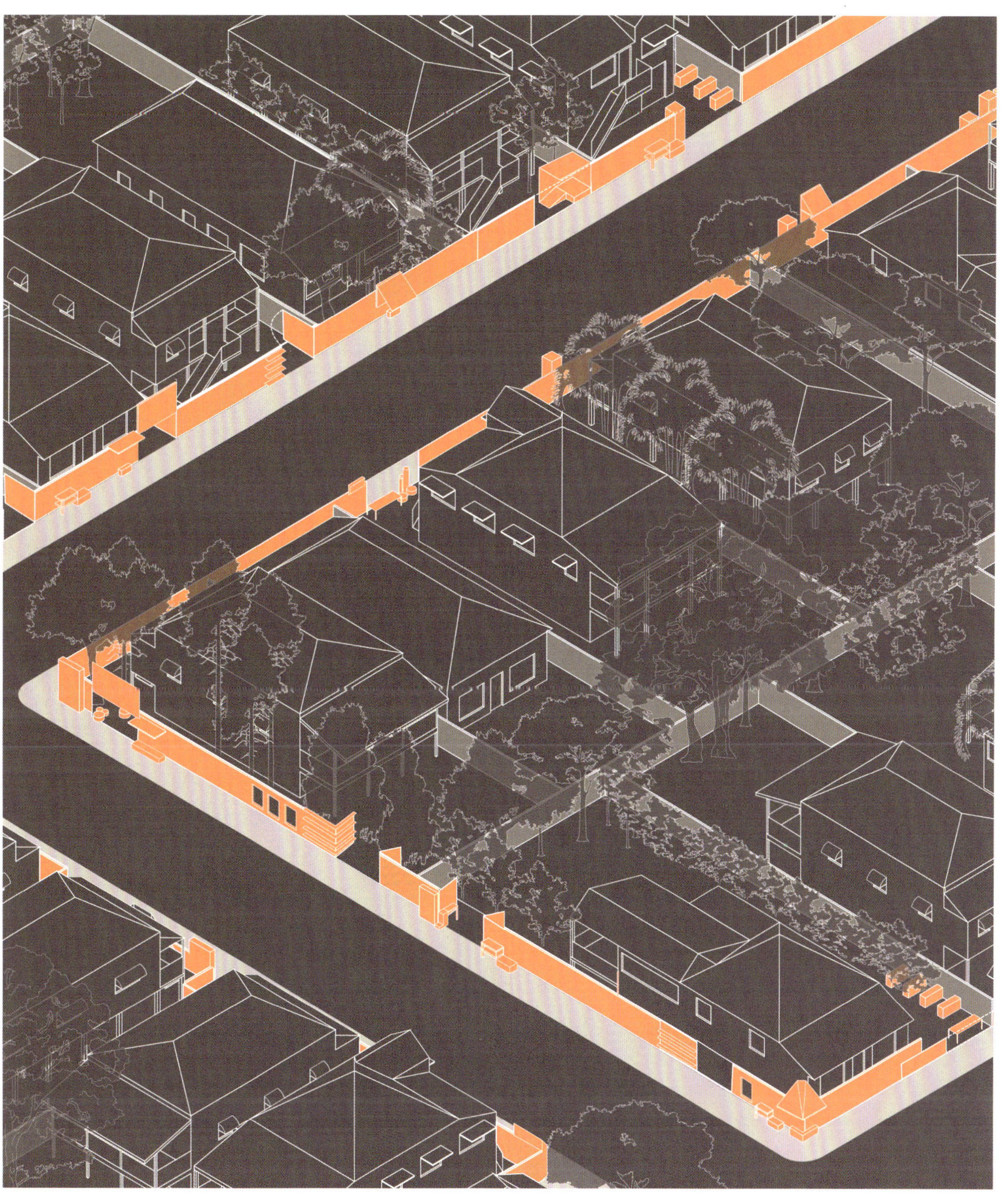

3.18 Installation model—2021 Melbourne Design Week.

Productive edge at the front of the house (Queenslander) serving as an access point to the undercroft productive/ workshop spaces.

From Consumption to Production

The notion of the productive edge has been tested in the speculative project House from Consumption to Production (2021),[22] aimed at transforming a dormant residential site located in the suburbs of Brisbane into a multifunctional space inclusive of productive activities [3.18]. The project interpolates two architectural initiatives. First, the building of a flexible pavilion, the One Room Tower (2018), designed in Brisbane by Phorm architecture + design with Silvia Micheli and Antony Moulis. And second, The Blue Bower (2021), a design research project undertaken by the same design team with The University of Queensland, exploring the activation of dormant edges in the cities of Seoul and Brisbane for the Global Studios at the 2021 Seoul Biennale of Architecture and Urbanism.[23]

House from Consumption to Production comprises a suite of design solutions to increase the productive potential of an existing Queenslander (timber house) and its multipurpose extension in the backyard, located on an assumed suburban site. Through strategic changes applied to the fence and underused spaces of the residential site, namely the Queenslander's open undercroft, back and front yards and sidewalks, this project proposes ways to turn the dormant areas into flexible and multifunctional ones. In doing so, the house shifts from a place predominated by consumption and entertainment to a dimension where production, display of items, and product exchange can simultaneously occur. The design proposition is an inventory of microscale interventions presented at diagrammatic level—strategies that supplement the existing house and that can be adapted to different architectural forms and configurations in the urban environment.

At the front of the Queenslander, a timber structure extends the edge of the veranda roof into a covered space for the arrival of materials to supply what could be a pottery studio or a workshop in the undercroft. This covered space commands a driveway access down below the building [3.19]. Beside it, a heightened balustrade located between the driveway and the stairs up onto the veranda contains a shelving box for the storage of materials arriving onsite. At the same time, this box can be thought of as ambiguous in its function: on occasion for the private use of the people resident onsite, as well as for storing goods. It also functions as a display site whereby local residents enter the property and can view and purchase things manufactured or handmade onsite.

Over at the site corner, reminiscent of Brisbane's traditional corner stores, the fence is raised and expanded volumetrically, with a platform on its interior side [3.20]. A sort of showcase, a rectangular cupboard operable from both

3.19 Detailed drawings—productive elements.

Design strategies to activate the edge of private property and its fence line such as a covered space and a shelving for the arrival and storage of materials on site. On the property's corner, the fence is raised and expanded volumetrically, with a platform on its interior side to display goods.

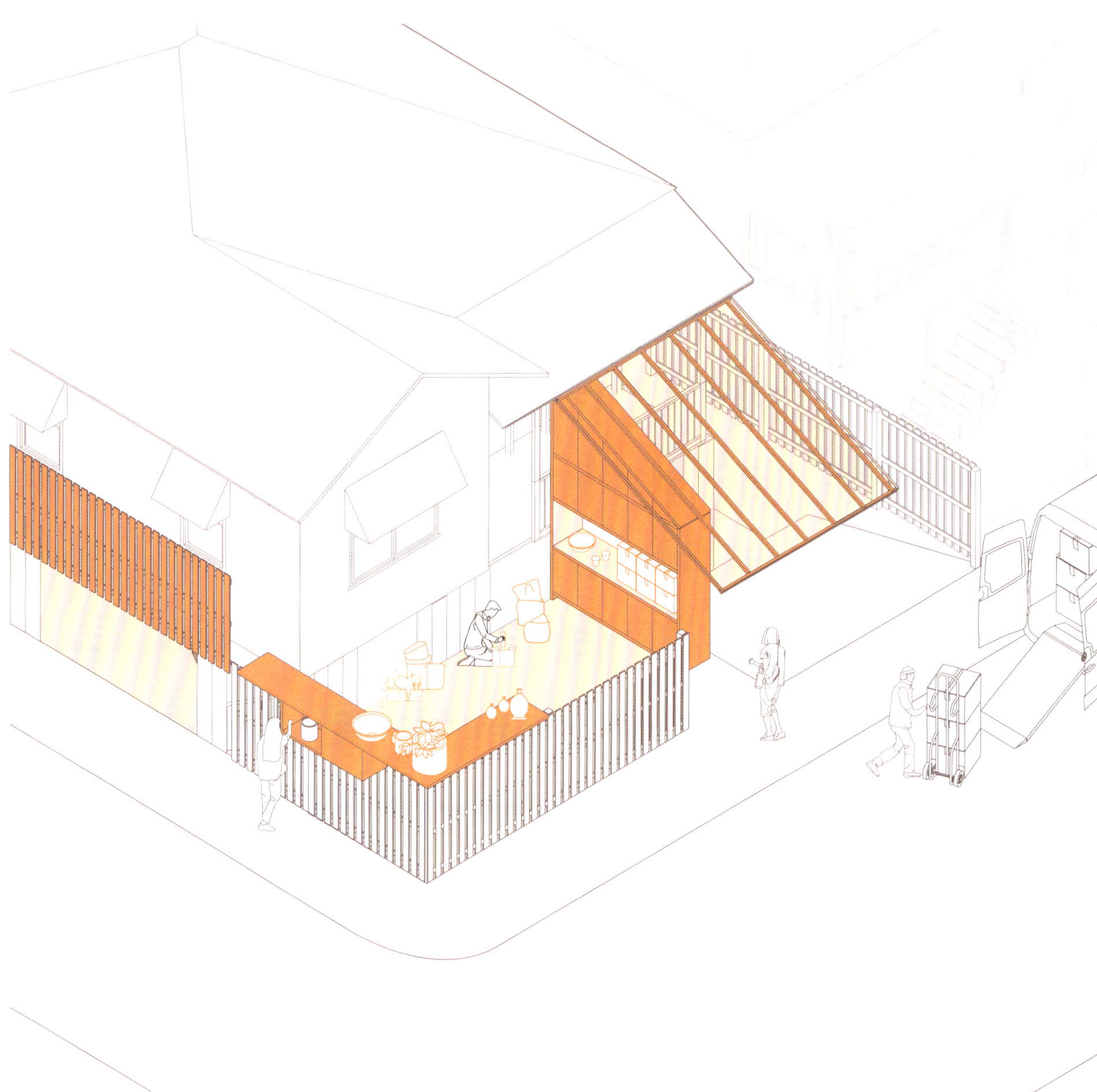

3.20 Installation model— Melbourne Design Week.

Design strategies to increase the use value and porosity of the fence line.

sides, connects the private property to the street, fully capturing our design thinking about the spatial idea and the formal potential of the productive edge. Local users can access the edge and inspect the cupboard openable from the inside and the outside at different times, adding autonomy and flexibility to a strategic point of encounter between private and public space. On top of the box is a shelf as the culmination of the fence, where residents can display goods. From the little platform behind the fence residents can raise themselves above the street and look out from this corner point to engage with passers-by.

Along the extended side street, the fence becomes a long edge, modified to admit views and access at different times. Here, the fence can be raised to provide visual and physical access into the productive space of the undercroft, equipped with tables for activities of production. The view into the productive spaces within the site invites people to engage in activities located in communities. Blurring the sheer distinction between public and private, spaces in residential properties are revealed beyond their conventional domestic dimension by de-constructing the enclosure.

The potentiality of the undercroft space is given by its entirely open nature [3.21]. There are a couple of ideas that flow from this. In the city, there is a tendency to enclose spaces under the house to create habitability, which contrasts their original use value as open, flexible spaces. Enclosure causes problems related to climate change, particularly in times of flood, which periodically affect the city, most recently in 2011 and 2022. Openness below the house allows any overland flow to move across the site, a practical aspect of the Queenslander's raising up on timber stumps. Openness also creates the possibility of changing uses in a space that is ordered discretely by the house's grid of stumps. Thus ultimately, the site boundary fence provides the enclosure of the property's spaces, inside which various productive activities can take place. Openness across the ground of the site allows the relationship of the house and the land to be revealed. The stepping of the land interacts with these platforms of production and sets up a chain of useable spaces.

In the backyard, the interstitial space between the Queenslander and the One Room Tower, which stand as two independent volumes, generates a miniature urban space between them and the street. Here is offered another variation of how the fence can be deployed on the edge. The fence can be swung open over a generous length, so the space between the pavilion and the house, typically private to the site, can reveal its productive dimension to the public. On the back of the site, on a rear laneway, there is a dual use addition of an elevated greenhouse that doubles as a street awning [3.22 and 3.23]. The idea of providing a shady edge out over the street also looks back to the idea of the corner store as a precedent, evoking the verandas that went out into the street to create structured public space.[24] While structuring the walkway,

3.21 Installation model—2021 Melbourne Design Week.

View to the undercroft repurposed as a site of production.

3.22 Installation model—2021 Melbourne Design Week.

The interstitial space between the Queenslander and the One Room Tower generates a miniature urban outdoor room interactive with the foothpath.

3.23 Detailed drawings— Productive elements.

The exploded axonometric shows the components of a sitting area and a plant nursery attached to the fence line providing shelter over the footpath.

the nursery provides shelter on the public ground, a solution that should be encouraged in a subtropical city such as Brisbane, where urban walkability is often undermined by harsh weather conditions. The greenhouse, occupied with propagated plants grown onsite that people can purchase, merges public functions with private domestic-scale productions. To envisage the edge in a productive way enhances the use value of the veranda itself and the potential for community engagement.

The productive edge enhances levels of public interaction, seeking to cut across conventionally understood and administered lines of governance that tend towards the segregation and separation of functions [3.24]. Through the appreciation of community-led actions in the everyday life of the city, we aim to inspire new practices that leverage on the hybrid nature of residential zones today, where suburban entrepreneurialism mixes work and living at a highly localised scale. Here, microbusinesses can play a significant role in facilitating flexible uses and soft transformations of the urban environment and developing connectivity within communities while, at the same time, seeding resilience [3.25].

3.24 Longitudinal section—Extending the productive edge.

Activation of a residential dwelling in Brisbane, along a chain of production.

3.25 Axonometric view— Extending the productive edge.

A series of elements added to the domestic site create the potential for flexible use—both public and private—as well as productive activities.

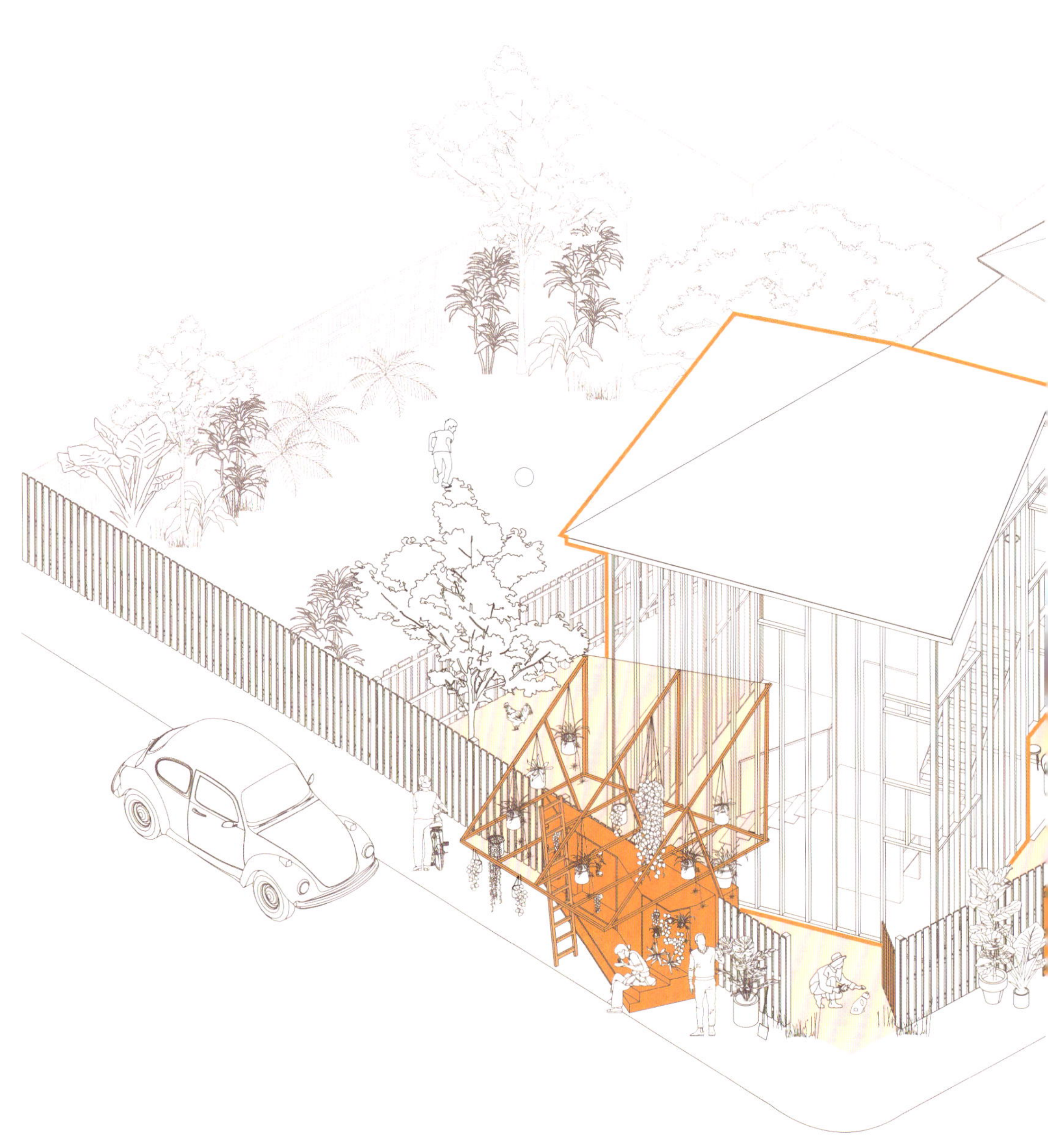

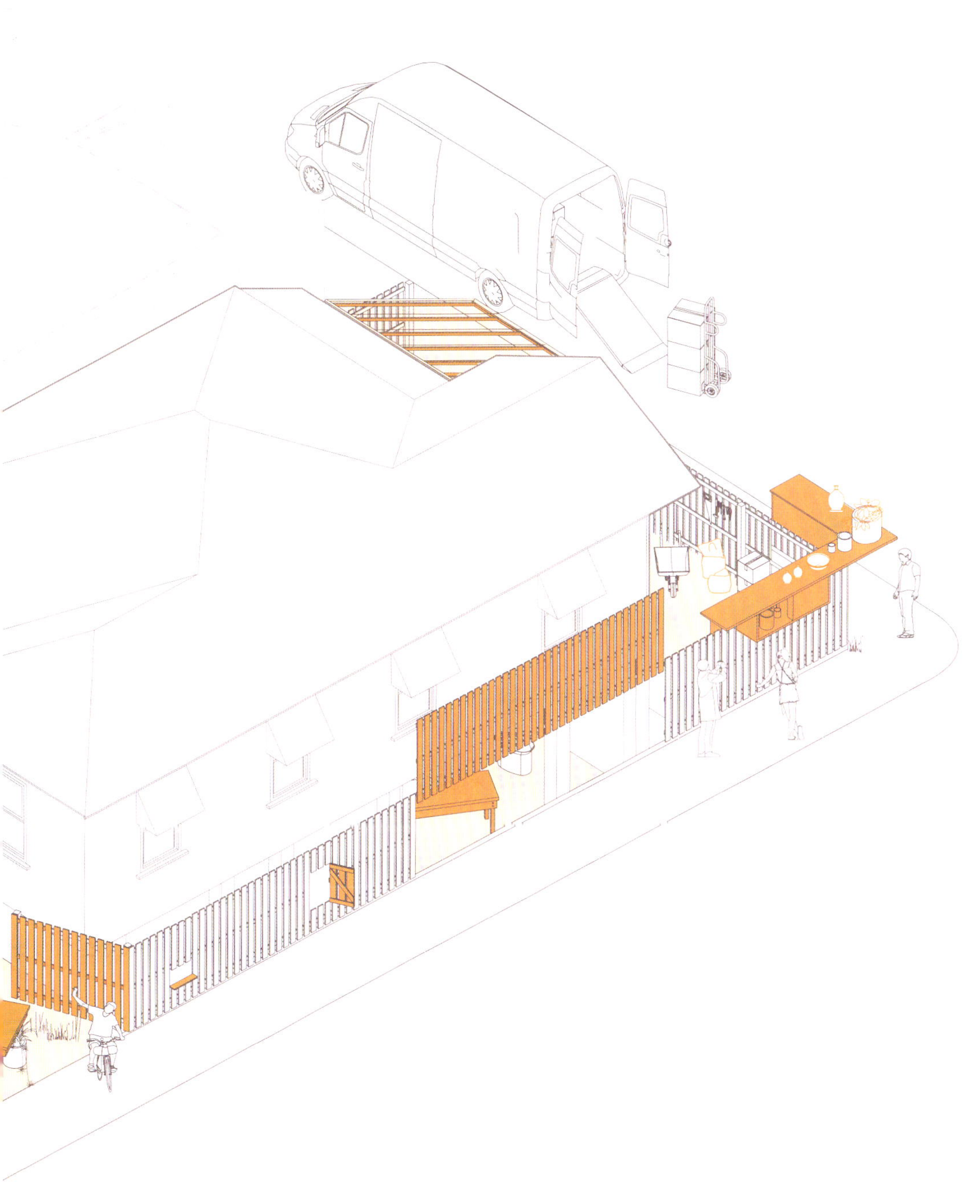

Endnotes

1. See Australian Bureau of Statistics. "Population." Last modified December 2022. https://www.abs.gov.au/statistics/people/population.
2. See European Council of Spatial Planners. "The New Leipzig Charter." Leipzig Charter 2020. 2020. https://ectp-ceu.eu/the-new-leipzig-charter/.
3. Xiao, Yijing, Burcin Becerik-Gerber, Gale Lucas, and Shawn C. Roll. "Impacts of Working from Home During COVID-19 Pandemic on Physical and Mental Well-Being of Office Workstation Users." Journal of Occupational and Environmental Medicine vol. 63, 3 (2021): 181–190.
4. Maginn, Paul J. and Gary Mortimer. "How COVID All But Killed the Australian CBD." The Conversation, October 30, 2020. https://theconversation.com/how-covid-all-but-killed-the-australian-cbd-147848.
5. Brisbane City Council mandates a setback of at least 1.5 metres on edges facing a secondary street and at least 3 metres facing a primary street. Rules and regulations regarding the required setbacks for residential dwellings can be found on the Brisbane City Council's official website at: https://www.brisbane.qld.gov.au/planning-and-building/do-i-need-approval/types-of-approval/building-near-the-boundary.
6. Stephens. K. "Perth to leapfrog Brisbane as third largest city in Australia." Brisbane Times. April 9, 2015, https://www.brisbanetimes.com.au/national/queensland/perth-to-leapfrog-brisbane-as-third-largest-city-in-australia-20150409.
7. For the connection between economic recession and the emergence of commercial spaces within residential sites see: Crawford, M. "Blurring the Boundaries: Public Space and Private Life", in Everyday Urbanism, edited by John Chase, Margaret Crawford, and John Kaliski. New York: Monacelli Press, 1999.
8. See Brisbane City Plan at https://www.brisbane.qld.gov.au/planning-and-building for zoning divisions.
9. Grimmer, L. and G. Mortimer. "More than milk and bread: corner store revival can rebuild neighbourhood ties." The Conversation. August 8, 2019, https://theconversation.com/more-than-milk-and-bread-corner-store-revival-can-rebuild-neighbourhood-ties-121244.
10. Hatuka, T. and E. Ben-Joseph. New Industrial Urbanism Designing Places for Production. Abingdon: Routledge, 2022.
11. Chase, John, Margaret Crawford, and John Kaliski. Everyday Urbanism. New York: Monacelli Press, 1999, 15.
12. Prominent critics of the 20th century, such as Henri Lefebvre, Jane Jacobs, Christopher Alexander, Guy Debord, and Michel de Certeau, according to different approaches, called for diversity and the inclusion of ordinary elements of daily life in design thinking and planning policy.
13. Ibidem, 10.
14. Ibidem, 8.
15. Bruno, M., S. Carena, and Min Ji Kim (MOTOElastico). Borrowed City. Seoul: DAMDI, 2013.
16. Zogolovitch, Roger. Shouldn't we all be Developers? London: Artifice, 2015.
17. Perez de Arce, Rodrigo. Urban Transformations and the Architecture of Additions. Abingdon: Routledge, 2014, 3.
18. Ibidem, 3.
19. See Haas, T., "New Urbanism & Beyond." in New Urbanism and Beyond: Contemporary and Future Trends in Urban Design, edited by Tigran Haas. New York: Rizzoli International Publications, 2008.
20. See Hou, Jeffrey. "(Not) your everyday public space." in Insurgent Public Space Guerrilla Urbanism and the Remaking of Contemporary Cities, edited by Jeffrey Hou. Abingdon: Routledge, 2010, and James Holston. "Spaces of Insurgent Citizenship." Planning Theory 13 (Summer 1996): 30–50.
21. Soja, Edward. Third space: Journeys to Los Angeles and Other Real and Imagined Places. New York: Basil Blackwell, 1996.
22. House from consumption to production in collaboration with Paul Hotston, director of Phorm Architecture + Design, was presented in the itinerant exhibition Making Tight, launched at the 2021 Melbourne Design Week with a 1:30 timber model on plinth at The University of Queensland Open Day in 2022 and in the November of the same year at the exhibition House, Precinct, Territory at the Domansa Urban Gallery in Seoul.
23. The Blue Bower Pavilion was designed by Phorm architecture + design with Silvia Micheli and Antony Moulis with the contribution of students from The University of Queensland. The core design team for the project consisted of Paul Hotston, Nicola White, Silvia Micheli, and Antony Moulis. The concept of the pavilion is underpinned by The Autonomous Edge project coordinated by Dr Silvia Micheli and Associate Professor Antony Moulis at The University of Queensland.
24. Brisbane retains a conspicuous number of well-preserved examples of this commercial tradition.

Dialogue with Remi Ayoko: The Productive House

This chapter is a transcript of a discussion between Associate Professor Remi Ayoko from The University of Queensland Business School and the members of the Productive Cities research team comprising Dr Silvia Micheli and Associate Professor Antony Moulis of The University of Queensland's School of Architecture; Dr Peyman Akhgar of Griffith University's School of Engineering and Built Environment; Dr John Doyle and Associate Professor Graham Crist at RMIT University's School of Architecture and Urban Design; and Dongwoo Yim and Dr Rafael Luna, co-founders of the architecture firm PRAUD. The group met via video conference on 7 November 2022 to discuss the topic of production in residential settings. The discussion ranged over economic and organisational issues, public governance and urban zoning, and the grassroots evolution of the contemporary productive house. The project proposition for a new suburban typology hybridising house and workplace and reimagining the domestic fence was debated, laying out key opportunities and challenges.

Silvia Micheli:
We have recently had discussions with Associate Professor Remi Ayoko from The University of Queensland Business School on a topic tangential to the discussion today. It involved how architecture intersects with emerging business models, so we thought that she is well-placed to join the conversation and bring her expertise with some ideas and reflections on our project. My first question is what do you think about the proposition we are putting forward concerning the relationship between the detached house and the productive dimension of the residential area?

Remi Ayoko:
This is a very good idea! I believe that the COVID-19 pandemic has shifted how we think about work and, more importantly, our thinking around workspaces. The pandemic has given us the idea that we can work from anywhere. You can see that right now in this meeting, we are meeting from around the world and, indeed, I am not actually in my office; I am at home. We can now begin to think about what happens when you have a suburban house and decide to pursue an entrepreneurial pathway from that house. The pandemic has allowed us to see the house as a site of business for those who do not want to be in an office or the central business district. That is the beauty of the whole concept.

Graham Crist:
During the COVID-19 lockdown in Melbourne, there was a stark difference in experience depending on the nature of your work: compare those who could easily work from home, like ourselves employed at universities, to those who were required to work onsite. This was reflected in our recent election, which highlighted the inequality of people in the knowledge classes compared to emergency and manufacturing workers. What are your thoughts about the difference between office work and manufacturing in terms of the domestic environment?

Remi Ayoko:
Recently, I had an opportunity to visit a manufacturing firm because I was looking at different workspaces with respect to the future of work. I asked those present about how a shift toward co-located or hybrid work will affect their business. The answer the manager gave me was, "Look, we're a manufacturing firm. We cannot let this equipment be taken home for people to use. They must come to work to do the manufacturing". So, for businesses or industries that engage in manufacturing, it is going to be very hard for them to work remotely. I can understand that when you have heavy equipment, you cannot easily shift it to the individual employee's environment. Similarly, if you are a doctor in a hospital, you need to be onsite to attend to the patients. So, the type of tasks you are engaged in would determine whether you can do your work from home.

Graham Crist:
We are interested in whether this sharp division can become blurry. In other words, is there a type of manufacturing that can bleed into the domestic environment? Or is there some modification of the domestic environment that can accommodate more manufacturing?

Remi Ayoko:
Yes, let me give you two examples. I am working at home today and I have a neighbour who, after 7 am, makes a lot of noise from his house. I suspect he is manufacturing something with metal. I haven't visited his house to see what it looks like, but I assume he has local council permission for this work. Also, across the road, I have neighbours who are bakers. I often visit the bakery at the front of their house to buy homemade cakes for morning tea. That's entrepreneurship in my suburb! These examples demonstrate that the division between working from home and from onsite locations can be managed depending on the type of manufacturing.

Antony Moulis:
In that respect, there are also the types of labour that occur within a single job position. If you are working for a larger organisation, there might be certain activities that you could do in your home and other activities that would require you to be present in other places. So, the gradation related to where work can be performed is starting to atomise.

Remi Ayoko:
Yes, there are a lot of nuances, and one solution cannot fit every scenario. So, if you are working at a company as an architect or designer, you might be able to take your design work home. But if you are at the point of physical production, then you may need to be at the manufacturing plant. The two tasks are very different and that is where the nuances come in.

Silvia Micheli:
This is a consideration of scale and the idea of diffused work. You can imagine a future where manufacturing is considered decentralised and some activities happen in a certain area while others defer to other parts of the city where zoning allows. So perhaps this notion of diffused work is useful to destabilise the division in centralised zoning and consider residential typologies that can host manufacturing activities. For instance, I do not think we necessarily have to have an end-to-end business activity located in the house, but the house can be deployed as part of the process. How do you see this idea from a business perspective?

Remi Ayoko:
In business management, we talk a lot about small businesses. In fact, in the last two semesters, I have asked my postgraduate students to study small business because more than 40 percent of workers that are employed in Australia right now are employed by small businesses. So, we need to pay attention to family businesses and allow opportunities for them to grow in the suburbs and serve their localised markets. This includes prioritising the design of homes to promote entrepreneurship.

John Doyle:
One of the interesting things about your observation, Remi, is the implications for urban and economic governance. A key reason why the government likes dealing with big business is that they have a single point of contact and an understanding of what the entity is and where it is located. They can create business districts with large-footprint buildings or plan manufacturing parks that are given over to one or several large organisations. When you begin talking about the prevalence of small businesses, you are talking about hundreds of thousands of entities all of which have different locations, addresses, scales, priorities, and business structures. So perhaps one of the challenges when we consider small business at the urban scale is considering the organisational models that allow for planning. I refer here to planning in the pure sense, like projecting for growth or change. How do we plan when we have so many different players?

Remi Ayoko:
I must qualify that my area of study is organisations and their behaviour, not strategic planning. However, I do know that when you start a business you conduct surveys to understand the demographics of your target market to inform your business plan. This information helps to build a scenario based on the economic activities that are happening now and then project that scenario into the future. In ten years, we are going to have the Olympics in Brisbane. There is already a lot of planning about who might be coming to the Olympics, their age, their ethnicity, their interests, and the kind of things they would expect from a host city. So, a lot of planning is happening right now, and I would imagine there will be a point where all that research can be brought together.

Graham Crist:
The Olympics is an interesting point because I know that Tokyo did their planning quite differently from previous cities insofar as they largely adapted existing facilities. Additionally, Tokyo planned to make up a large proportion of its accommodation not through new hotels but using models such as Airbnb. This contrasts with the massive, centralised nation-building projects when they hosted the games 50 years earlier. So, it is not the same issue necessarily, but the Tokyo 2020 Olympics is an example of how the post-industrial city might be better set up for adaptive reuse and alteration at the very fine grain.

Antony Moulis:
I want to return to the issue that was raised about scale. When you are working at the scale of a suburban house, you are looking at the actions of individuals or small groups. When considering concepts of sustainability and resilience, we are asked as individuals to do small actions to help tackle a larger problem. For example, the way that we recycle in our home is a small action that if we all did, contributes to a larger identified goal.

Remi Ayoko:
Most of the time, when people talk about sustainability, we think, "That's the government's responsibility". But sustainability is a multi-level problem. So, it is not only at the societal and governmental level but also, as you say, it is the responsibility of the individual. Issues of sustainability must consider carbon footprint, transportation, and noise. In your project scenario, I am imagining that once businesses are brought out of the central business district and into the suburbs, traffic will be heavy. This will raise issues of increased noise and a large carbon footprint for the area. Architects will need to consider this as a major challenge. I am concerned about this as my research is usually around distractions and noise. As I said, my neighbour makes noise occasionally and I have to put something in my ears when I am working from home. I wish he had a house where noise could be contained without disturbing the neighbourhood. I am all for businesses within the suburbs, but without noise—if that is possible!

Rafael Luna:
This raises an interesting design issue. If you are working from a suburban house, the tendency would be to use excess space of the home to produce small-scale entrepreneurial ventures. So, like your earlier example of the baker, their business is restricted by the amount of leftover space in the house. The interesting thing about using the residual space of the home is that you do not need a permit because the predominant use is residential. However, as soon as you give over more space for industrial production, it takes on a different planning code. Because of this, I think house-based businesses are always restricted to small ventures and I don't think they will ever get to something of a bigger scale.

Remi Ayoko:
I agree with you on many fronts. However, the points you raised depend on which country you are in. In Australia, I think you do need permission to run a business at home, in the same way as you need permission to add a new fence or put a pool at the back of your house. Also, there is the issue of territoriality. I study territoriality in the context of the office, and I can translate it to this issue. When we are talking about territoriality, we are saying, "This is mine and you can't touch it". You see this happen in the suburbs over the issue of fences. Neighbours fight because a fence has moved an inch one way or another. These are territorial behaviours, and we must consider how we can manage them when business activities are taking place in the suburbs.

John Doyle:
The fence dispute Remi mentioned is almost the cliché of the Australian suburb! In practice, I have built several projects that have been more or less seamless through planning and construction until the fence is constructed at the end and that is the point at which the neighbours have almost come to blows. Modifying the fence holds great opportunities as the "House: From Consumption to Production" project shows, but also appreciable challenges.

Antony Moulis:
There's a question of how an architectural brief is constructed and responding to cultural assumptions around how people think about living and working. As you say, in different countries there would be different cultural expectations around noise levels near places of living or different concerns about site boundaries and aesthetics in an urban context. So, the question refers to that regulatory environment, but also how, through architectural experimentation, you might be able to anticipate a shift in cultural assumptions because of the value that you can bring by creating new possibilities for business activities in the house.

Graham Crist:
The restriction of the size of the enterprise is partly a design question. There are plenty of examples where people start to scale up their business within the suburban envelope. I'm thinking of a Vietnamese friend who grew chillies at a commercial scale, but entirely within his suburban garden. There was no permit required and no nuisance to neighbours. There was nothing except an extreme efficiency of the garden; it was growing from fence to fence, and the scale of it was enough to generate income.

John Doyle:
One aspect to pivot towards quickly, with a view of your expertise Remi, is the issue of finance. One of the things that prevents the construction of non-house types in suburbia is financing and lending. Banks lend on houses. There is a colloquial expression in Australia that something is as safe as houses if it is a safe investment. If, for example, you wanted to buy a shop front and convert it into a house, often a bank will not lend the money until they are completely satisfied that it can be converted into a house. The lending criteria for different typologies are quite different. Do you see any kind of issues or opportunities within

the financing of a business that could either catalyse or prevent its production in suburbia?

Remi Ayoko:
Yes, lenders are looking for profit. Banks lend money so they can deliver wealth to their shareholders. They are concerned about whether they will generate enough profit if they sell the house tomorrow. If they believe people will not buy the house because, for instance, it has specific features related to the business it contains, then the banks will not lend on that basis. Perhaps that explains why banks are sluggish in giving money to people who want an atypical house typology. The other issue is insurance. The bank will be slow to lend money if they know insurance will not cover the house because of the way it is designed or used. We are in a trial period, but once we have these kinds of houses in place and organisations can see that more people are wanting to buy such houses, I imagine there will be a revision of insurance policies and lending criteria.

John Doyle:
What about microfinance? In emerging economies there are microfinancing schemes that allow small businesses to be set up as part of poverty alleviation. It is a different conversation in a very wealthy country like Australia, but do you think the central government or other not-for-profit agencies can play a role in shaping the suburbs through microfinancing schemes for small suburban businesses?

Remi Ayoko:
If there is a need for it, then I do not see any reason why the government should not be able to finance it because the government is not set up for profit. They are concerned with providing infrastructure for people so they can have a better quality of life. So, if the government can see that microlending will alleviate poverty and improve wellbeing, then they should be microfinancing the types of projects we are talking about.

Peyman Akhgar:
Just a quick question about the benefits of microbusinesses. What do you think is the value of domestic production in the resiliency of the city in general? Or rather, what is the role of these small businesses in the formal economy?

Remi Ayoko:
Small business, or entrepreneurship, is about creativity. In the western world, we pride ourselves on allowing people to be creative and seeing how that can mesh with economic growth. Creating opportunities for people to flexibly manage their home and business is allowing people to experiment. For example, perhaps I am a seamstress, and I don't have enough money to rent a shop. I am happy to work in my house without creating any disadvantages for my neighbours. The government should allow me to do that. This issue is also about reducing risk. Small businesses involve a lot of risk, particularly when your family depends on an income. By giving people the opportunity to test business ideas in their homes, we are giving them a low-risk environment to explore their creativity and see whether their business is sustainable.

Peyman Akhgar:
Regulations can affect opportunities for those people operating home businesses. For example, there are limits on the visual connection and signage that is allowed on the street to advertise a home business and restrictions on the number of visitors who can attend because of car parking. So, I think this issue goes back to the question of councils and their zoning practices.

Remi Ayoko:
I understand that. In business, we always talk about top management support. There is nothing you can do in business that will materialise if your top management does not support you. There must be governance. The people who are governing the organisation or the city must support the idea.

Dongwoo Yim:
I was wondering whether this phenomenon of running a small business out of the suburban home is, or will be, a worldwide phenomenon in the post-COVID-19 era.

Remi Ayoko:
It will be more challenging in the western world because of the regulations we have just noted. Some people want to dissociate work from home while others are happy to work from home. These are two separate modes, but clearly today the emphasis is still generally on separating homelife from the workplace, and this is clearly reflected in the regulatory environment. But moving forward, people who want to design their homes in such a way that they can carry out their business should be allowed to do so. I think in the next 10 years, we will begin to see more of this happening around the world.

Silvia Micheli:
I understand this model of working in one place and living in another, but don't you think it is also a construct that is being imposed upon us? Going back to the beginning of our conversation, one of the positive things that happened to our society through the difficult COVID-19 period was seeing a different model where working from home is not necessarily bad. It can save you a lot of time, give you proximity to your family, and allow you to contribute to the economy of your neighbourhood. I am convinced that there will be a shift because now we are too aware of what working from home can entail and for some people there is a large benefit.

Remi Ayoko:
There is certainly a tension around working from home. You have just told me all the positive aspects, but for others it is confining and negatively impacts wellbeing. It's paradoxical: good for some people and not so good for others. Nonetheless, the government has a responsibility to look after all of us. Part of this is how work and home are demarcated within the house. Separating the uses will help some people, but we must acknowledge that for others it will be very difficult. The entrepreneurs who are open to this new way of working and who can manage that interface reveal new opportunities. With the satisfaction of combining work and home can come improved wellbeing and increased income, making suburban life more vibrant and connected. That is the way I'm looking at it.

Graham Crist:
That is a nice way to conclude things: the happy suburb.

Remi Ayoko:
I hope that when these ideas take place in reality, there will be an opportunity for us to meet our neighbours whom we have never met before. And of course, when you have more social interactions, people are happier.

Silvia Micheli:
A positive note on which to end. Thank you so much, Remi.

2
PRECINCT

(Seoul)

Rafael Luna
Dongwoo Yim

Loose Accesories for a Tight Urbanity

Cities need platforms where plurality of amenities and services can coexist within a single structure.

Density can be a catalyst for the development of ad-hoc solutions for sustaining urban life. While some bottom-up solutions address the need for services and amenities to be distributed where needed, they may appear as illegal human appropriations of space. Yet, they also serve as clues for how architecture can also manifest these needs through spatial solutions.

During the 10th World Urban Forum in 2020, convened by UN-Habitat, an international goal on urbanisation was established.

"The increasing recognition of the importance of towns and cities was reflected in the introduction of Sustainable Development Goal 11—the cities goal—to make cities inclusive, sustainable, resilient, and safe by 2030."[1]

This global goal reinforces city initiatives like the *15-Minute City* in Paris,[2] or the *Supermanzana* in Barcelona,[3] which aim at supplying each citizen with amenities within a walking radius from where they live for a more sustainable and equitable city. For the megacity of Seoul, the project *Sharing City*[4] was announced in 2022 as an initiative to explore sharing economies aided by technology. The project is highly contextual to the fourth industrial revolution topics such as artificial intelligence automation, mass customisation, decentralisation, and circular economies. These are perhaps topics of engineering and economics that question the role of architecture within this technological framework. While the sharing economy has been building its presence through virtual interfaces, the physical reality is that cities need platforms where a plurality of amenities and services can coexist within a single structure. Resources can be further optimised by understanding how architecture and the built environment can respond to these initiatives to produce more dynamic and inclusive neighbourhoods.

Mixed programmatic environments have become more relevant in the last few years due to a series of unforeseen, unpredictable events (commonly called black swan events) that halted supply chains globally. The COVID-19 disease global pandemic lockdowns, followed by the blocked Suez Canal due

4.1 Streetview in Seongsu-dong.

Pedestrians and vehicles share the same public space.

to the grounding of the container ship *Ever Given*, harmed production and distribution across the globe, putting a great deal of pressure on local economies. The Russo–Ukrainian war is threatening global energy and food production networks. As a macroeconomic trend, the world is already in a transition towards de-globalisation,[5] and these black swan events have sped up the process, making the need for local production (consumer goods, commodities, energy, and food) more evident. While the black swan theory states that these events were unpredictable, not adhering to any reasonable trend of history or science at first glance, in hindsight their cause could be traced. This means that although there is a slim chance to predict the next disruptive event, cities can take measures to be more resilient and adaptable.

The demographics of Seoul add to the imminent problem of implementing localised production and supply chains. It is projected that by the year 2050, the population of Seoul will be 7,918,861 [6] of which 4,149,844 [7] people will be over the age of 65. Seoul will be a super-aged society with a retired population, and a lack of productive workforce, a condition that will be similar in other aging nations, such as Japan or Germany. These macro trends are pushing for more dynamic, flexible, equitable, and sustainable environments, requiring architecture to re-evaluate how to produce transformable and resilient spatial systems.

In the highly dense urban settings of Seoul, mixed-use programming has developed naturally in most neighbourhoods. Buildings are congested with commercial programs such as retail, offices, and markets, mixed with residential and educational facilities. This can be seen, for the most part, throughout Seoul. [4.1].

The root of this condition can perhaps be traced to the 1960s when Oswald Nagler, who had studied under Josep Lluís Sert at Harvard, was invited to Korea by the Asian Foundation to review the state of urbanisation.[8] Nagler introduced concepts like the Linear City and Clarence Perry's concept for the neighbourhood unit. The neighbourhood unit was based on the population that one elementary school could sustain, as a block type. Each neighbourhood unit was self-contained in a 500–800 metre width, a dimension that derived from an understanding of minimum dwelling units and their aggregation. The ideas were presented in the Housing, Urban, and Regional Planning Institute (HURPI) exhibition of 1967 in Seoul, and influenced young architects and planners in Korea.[9] Despite mixed use being ingrained in Seoul's urban fabric, mixing production inside the city limits is restricted to certain areas. In 2011, manufacturing only represented 7.4 percent of the businesses in Seoul and 6.1 percent of the workforce.[10]

"The top 5 manufacturing areas in Seoul in 2011, determined based on the number of businesses, were found to be the manufacturing of sewn clothing and fur products (23.8%), publishing, printing and recorded media reproduction (12.6%), manufacturing of assembly metal products (10.2%), manufacturing of food and beverage (9.7%) and manufacturing of furniture and other products (9.6%). The number of businesses in these areas were shown to account for 65.9% of the total number of businesses in the entire manufacturing industry." [11]

As seen in the Special Purpose Area map of 2012,[12] industry is mainly limited to the fringe areas of Seoul. [4.2]. There is a larger area that runs continuously through Yeongdeungpo, Yangpyeong, Mullae, Sindorim, Guro, and Gasan. The largest single standing area is Seongsu-dong, on the eastern side of Seoul. This is a neighbourhood that thrives in diversity, mixing industry alongside residences and commerce.

"In the 2030 Seoul Plan, Seongsu is defined as a regional centre. The main roles of the regional centers consist in strengthening self-sufficiency by living area and facilitating the improvement of the quality of life by activating commerce and business functions based on regional characteristics."[13] [4.3].

4.2 Special-purpose Areas, 2012.

Zoning map of Seoul.

4.3 Building Function Mapping.

Buildings in the semi-industrial zoning of Seongsu-dong.

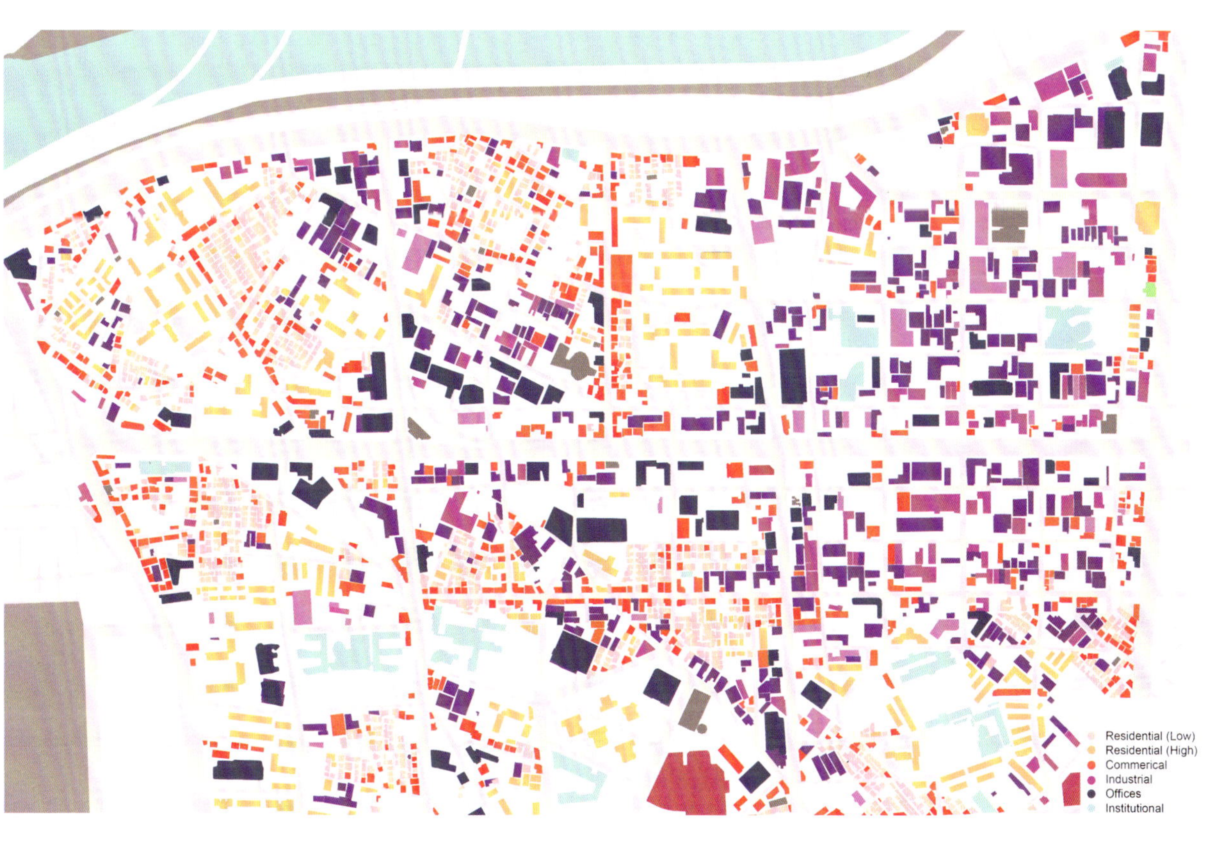

Seongsu has the particular characteristic of mainly being associated with the shoe industry, as well as other light industries that are nestled between blocks. Some factory buildings have been transformed into cafes that attract visitors to the neighbourhood, as the mixture of building typologies produces a unique urban environment. [4.4]. Blocks, varying in sizes and building compositions, are mixed even within themselves. Yet, the diversity in Seongsu is not typologically facilitated by extravagant new buildings, but by banal and ordinary modern buildings. Through a deeper survey of the urban fabric, we could acquire a more detailed understanding of its vernacular characteristics that are facilitating a sustained polycultural environment.

A survey was conducted in 2019 between Ttukseom Station and Seongsu Station in an area of about 1.5 kilometre squared, mainly north of the green line where urban factories are mixed between residential and commercial buildings. Initially, the urban factories were catalogued to study their individual morphology. [4.5]. These functioning urban factories present a unique architectural characteristic of being non-factory typologies that have been converted to facilities of production by attaching industrial elements to existing buildings. [4.6]. Most factories were in banal, modern buildings that have been adapted with vents and ducts cascading through the façade. Some had additional electrical transformers on the roof to operate heavy machinery inside. Others attach lifts, cranes, and elevators to the side of the building to move materials vertically along the exterior of the building. [4.7]. Oversized doors or windows have been carved into the façade of some buildings for easy material access. These building alterations can be classified through elements within an architectural language. These elements are not traditional architectural elements, but borrowed ready-made industrial elements that enhance the performance of a specific program. This survey indicated that the building stock within the urban fabric could be composed through generic modern systems, regardless of the program, and through the use of specific elements of buildings that could change their use, performance, and appearance, while maintaining the same underlying modern system.

On a closer look at other buildings around this neighbourhood, the same condition of attaching elements to existing buildings was found for commercial, retail, symbolic, civic, and residential buildings. There is an inherent flexibility in the neighbourhood, which has a rapid turnover of tenants. Commercial tenants can quickly change businesses within a building by attaching temporary façades that would cover the original façade of the building. These façades are ornamental and serve the purpose of beautification, with no utilitarian motive. These ornamental elements would also be seen in combination with other programs. Other commercial buildings use signs that indicate the plurality of programs happening inside the building. Some signs use text, while others use a symbolic form such as a

4.4 Photo of Shoe Steet in Seongsu-dong.

Micro-shops allow visitors to see the manufacturing process and purchase the handmade shoes.

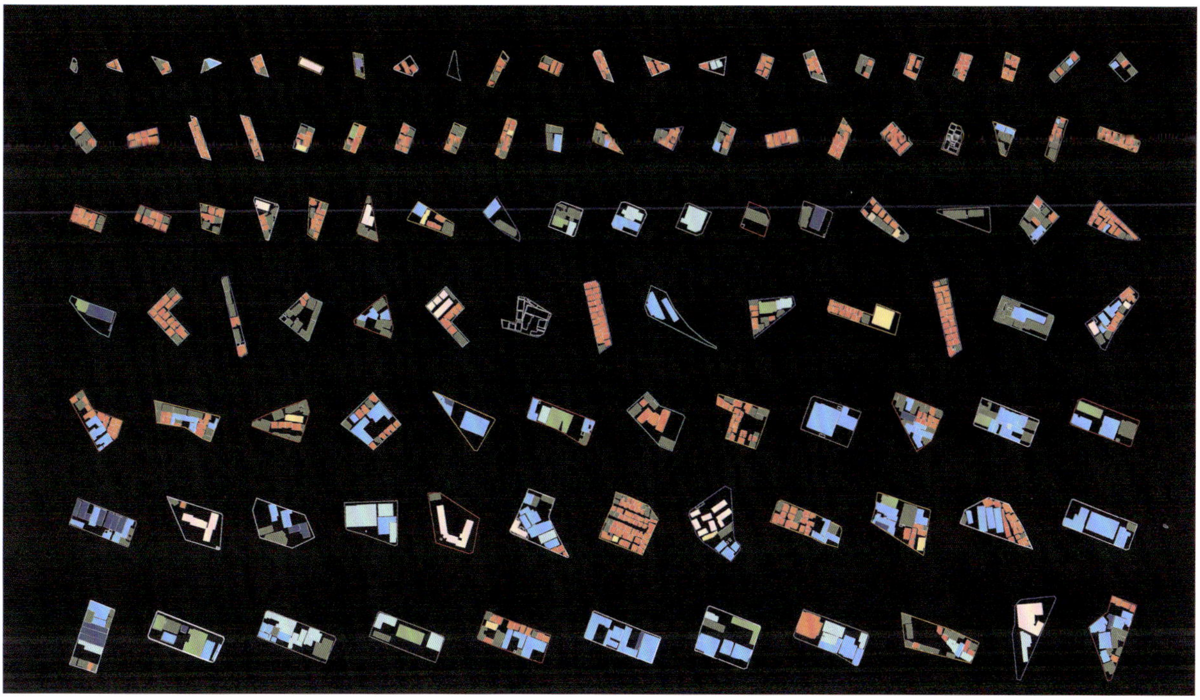

4.5 Urban Morphologies.

Mapping of different block typologies and their programming in Seongsu-dong.

4.6 Urban Factories.

Typologies of factory buildings in Seongsu-dong.

4.7 Attachments

Different element attachments and mutations on modern buildings.

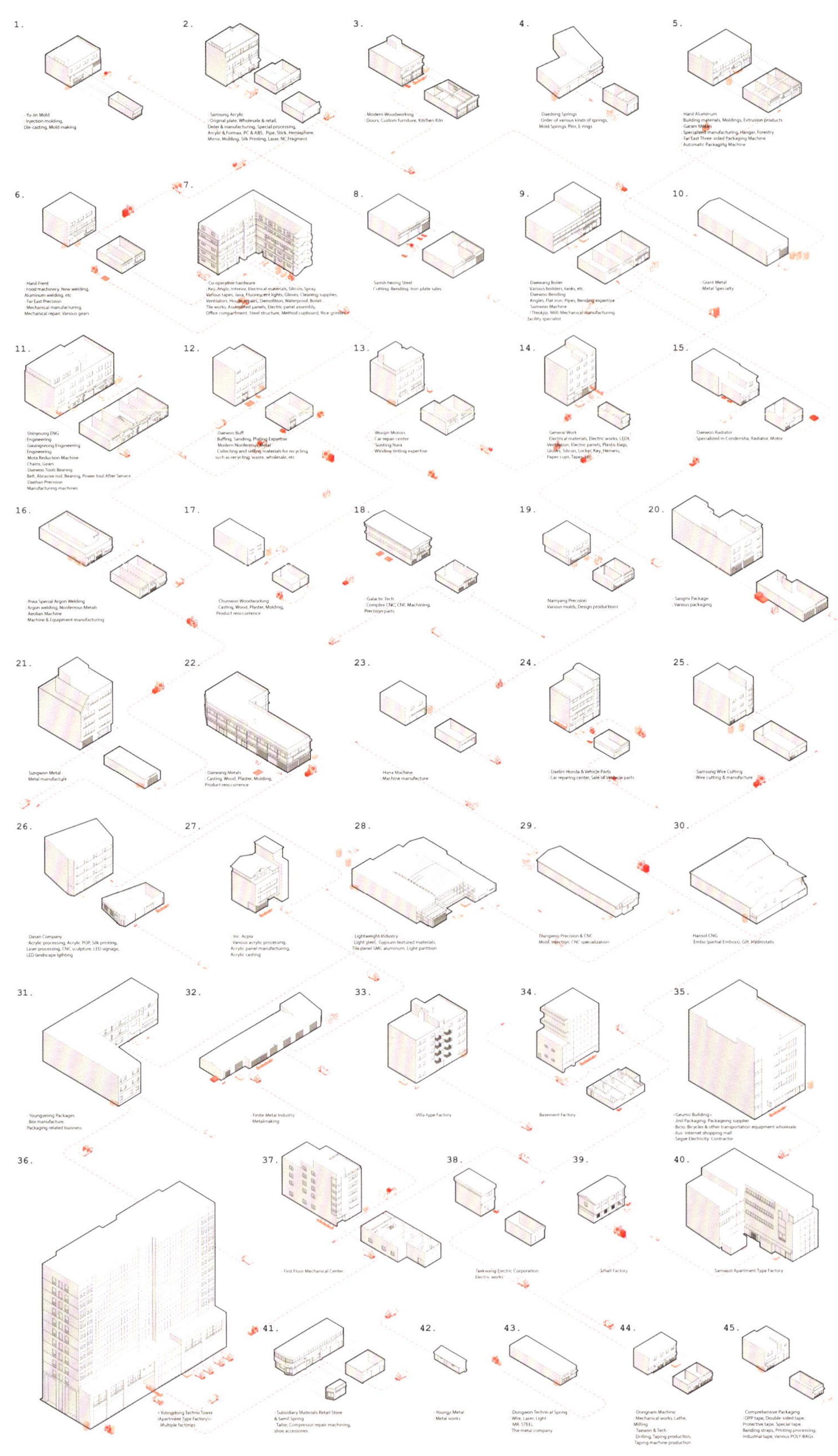

삼영 문화

팅

FedEx

4.8 Productive Elements. Axon of attached elements found in urban factories in Seongsu-dong.

cross on a turret to indicate there is a church inside. These are semiotic elements. Finally, some buildings extended their space using spatial elements such as canopies, roofs, and façade extensions. Through the examples found in the survey of Seongsu, we can classify four categories of elements that are used to optimise the building, yet are not necessarily architectural. These are spatial, ornamental, semiotic, and performative elements. Having found these ready-made attachments generates a new perspective on the role of elements in architecture, perhaps as a way to achieve flexible systems through a new category labelled productive elements. [4.8]. Despite the elements found being non-architectural, each of the four categories can be explained through a lineage of architectural theory that makes them relevant for consideration within the field as an adaptive reuse strategy to retrofit buildings and neighbourhoods.

Spatial Elements

Informal structures provide clues on how an element can play multiple roles, and different environments could be produced from a singular spatial element.

An initial theoretical standpoint on elements can be associated with Marc-Antoine Laugier's Primitive Hut from his book, *An Essay on Architecture*.[14] [4.9]. Laugier hypothesises the production of architecture through rudimentary components. He imagines a narrative where a primitive man, left in the wild, would instinctively seek shelter. First, he would seek the shade under the canopy of a tree, which would not protect him against the wind. He would then move inside a cave, but the bad air and light quality make it unlivable, long term. Eventually, he would build a shelter by assembling branches into a square formation with other branches forming a triangle on top. The vertical branches can be conceptualised as columns, the horizontal branches on top of the columns work as an entablature, and the branches that form a triangle on the roof of the hut would be a pediment. This, he mentions, are the basic elements for any piece of architecture.

"I conclude then with saying, in all the order of architecture, there is only the column, the entablature, and the pediment that can essentially enter into this composition. If each of these three parts are found placed in the situation and with the form which is necessary for it, there will be nothing to add; for the work is perfectly done."[15]

Laugier was imagining a Greek or Roman composition of architecture, classical in the sense that it forms a basic foundation for all other architecture to follow, and these three components (column, entablature, and pediment) are the essential elements. Other components like doors and windows are essential elements to make the space habitable, but are of a second order.

Although Laugier's essay is from the mid-18th century, it establishes a reading of architecture through its kit of parts. In developing countries, the primitive hut is a vivid example of ad-hoc environments that are made through a rudimentary composition of spatial elements. Found pieces of construction materials are placed together to produce enclosures and collective informal settlements. If we borrow from Laugier's logic of looking at the primitive hut

4.9 The Primitive Hut.

Frontispiece for Laugier's Essay on Architecture.

4.10 The Vernacular Hut.

Hut for a roadside vendor, built out of sticks and straw.

4.11 Spatial Element, Shed.

Diagrams of a shed structure in Seongsu.

4.12 Spatial Element, Canopy.

Diagrams of a canopy structure in Seongsu.

as the foundation of architecture, we can look at these informal structures as a way of understanding that an element can play multiple roles, and different environments could be produced from a singular spatial element. [4.10].

In essence, spatial elements are the components that form the space such as columns and beams, but they can also be conceptualised as compound components. In Seongsu, for example, factories extend their capacity by using shed structures. [4.11]. These are light structures that form a roof over a residual space in order to have an additional usable area not originally intended by the building's program, producing an additional flexible space. The shed, in itself, can be understood as a singular element that can be plugged into void spaces, despite the shed having different assembly parts. The same applies for micro-shops that can fit in the sidewalk to in-between urban spaces.

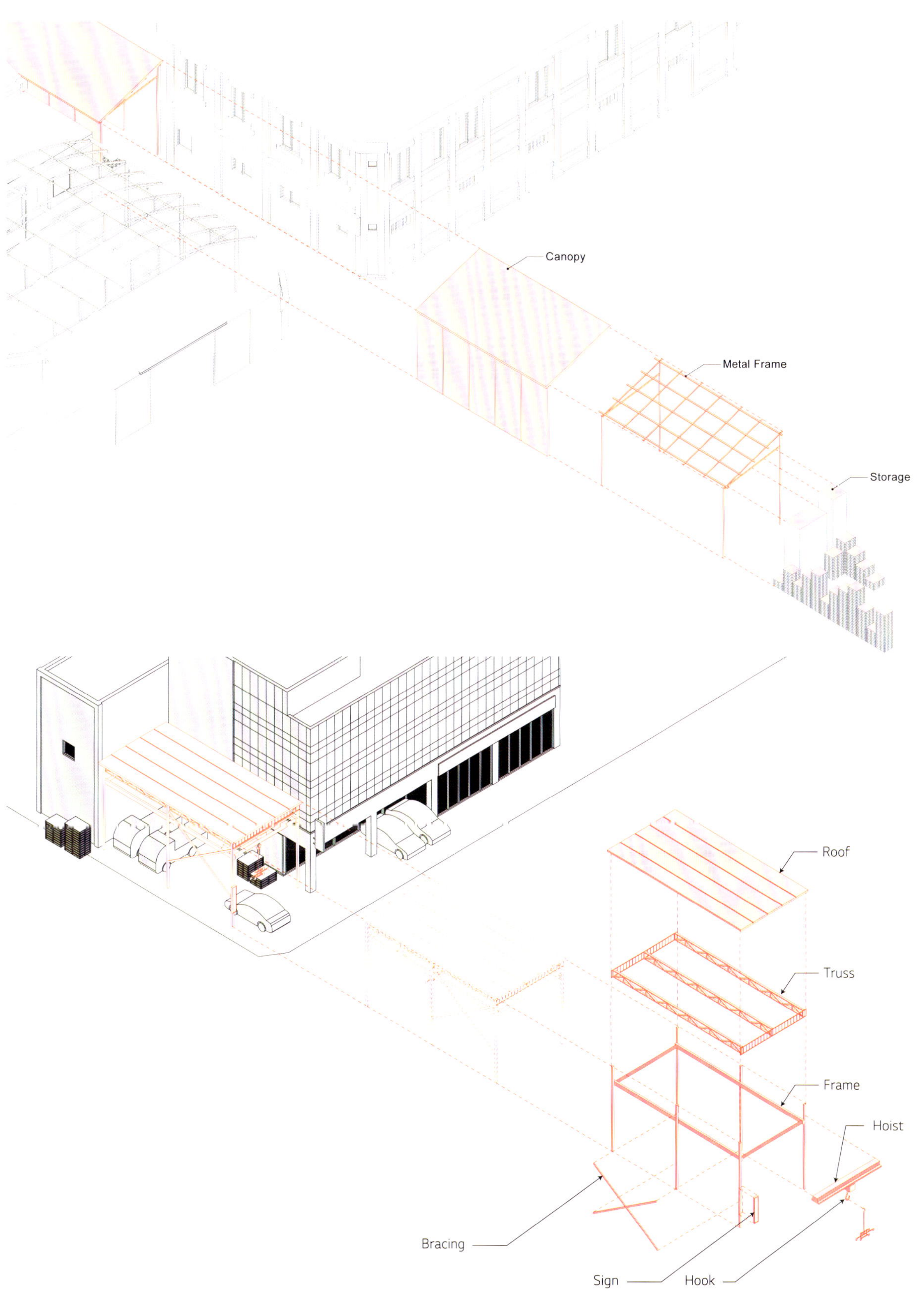
Canopy
Metal Frame
Storage
Roof
Truss
Frame
Hoist
Bracing
Sign
Hook

Ornamental Elements

The ornament has maintained a discretionary role in architecture as it is debatably an ad-on.

In 1795, Jean-Nicolas-Louis Durand was appointed to the Ecole Polytechnique in Paris to teach architecture to engineering students.[16] In order for his engineering students to learn architecture within a limited time, Durand wrote a series of lessons that synthesised the way of understanding architecture through its elements. He pointed to the inefficacies of the usual way of teaching architecture by separating it into decorations, distribution, and construction, as it would not have been possible to teach this way within the timeframe he was given. Instead, Durand focused on the efficiency and economy of compositional elements. He systematised a selective process of plans, sections, and elevations through a rational approach that discarded decorations and ornamentation from the process of architecture.

The ornament has maintained a discretionary role in architecture as it is debatably an ad-on. In *The Function of the Ornament*,[17] Mousavi and Kubo criticise the role of the architect as a façade designer due to the scale of buildings being developed, which disassociate the shell from the interior to optimise the economics of the interior space. This phenomenon has produced ornamental façades that function independently of the structure and interior space logic. Yet, for Seongsu, buildings are transformed through a process of decoration, a masquerading of the building in order to provide multiple uses. This is done through secondary fake façades that are attached to the original building. [4.13]. Just like a selection from the précis of Durand, tenants select façades that are added onto the building to transform microenvironments (storefronts, markets, educational institutions) within a single building. These are ornamental elements that, for the most part, serve an aesthetic function.

Modernism dictated the separation of the façade from the primary structure, treating the façade as a singular element that could be designed on its own. [4.14 and 4.15]. The façade, under modernism, is already an ornamental element that can be replaced, exchanged, and transformed over time. Under that premise, retrofitting modern buildings with flexible spaces through the

4.13 Seoul Masquerade.

Photos of attached fake façades.

4.14 Building Masquerade 1.

Diagram of fake façade components.

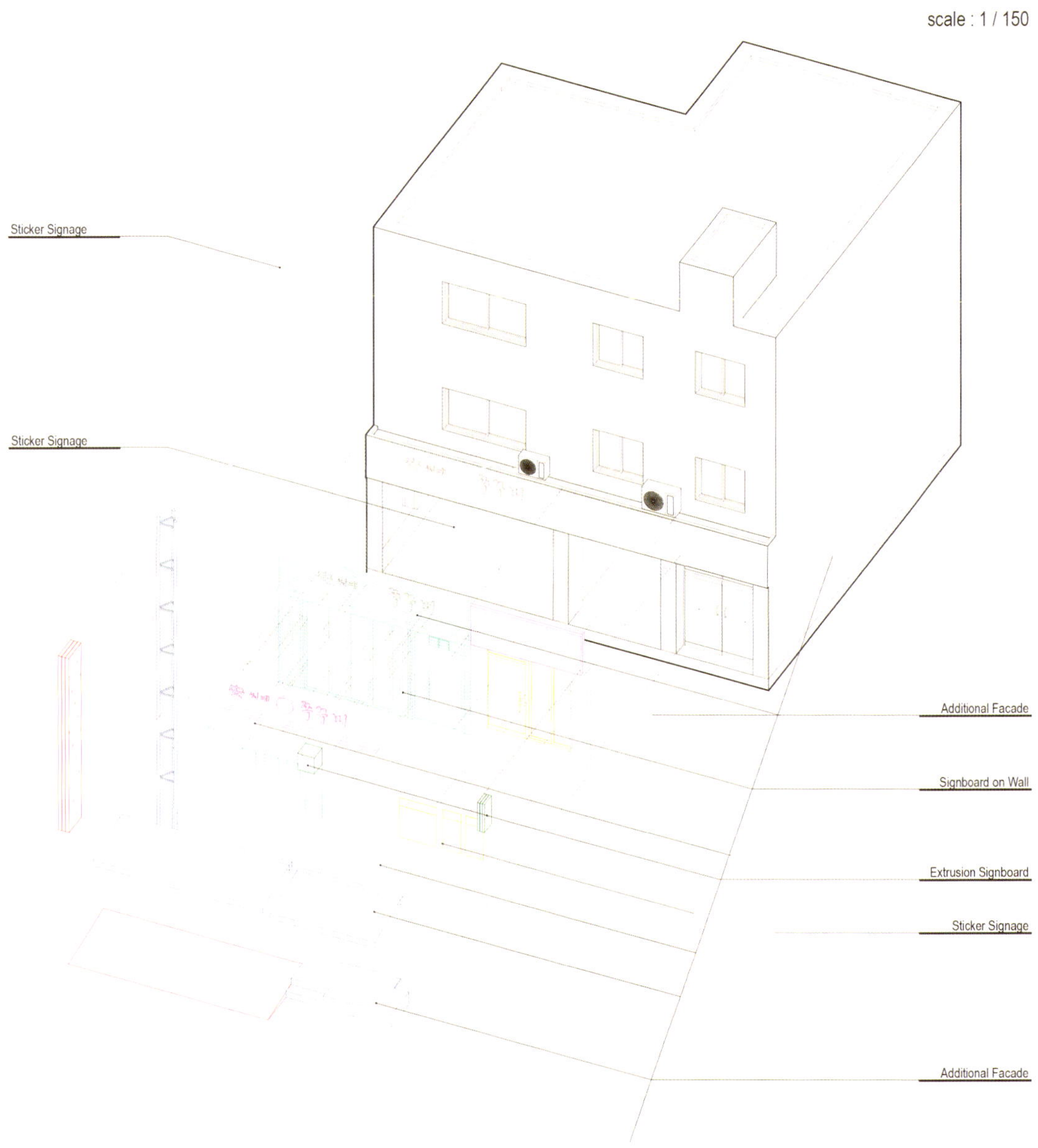

scale : 1 / 150
Sticker Signage
Sticker Signage
Additional Facade
Signboard on Wall
Extrusion Signboard
Sticker Signage
Additional Facade

Building Height : 18.4m
Building Storeys: 6 / 1 (Above Ground / Underground)
Commercial Usage : 5 / 1
Area :

Appraised Value of Land : About $19,333/㎡ (2019)

~ 1500 ~ 1000 ~ 400 ~ 100 ~ 10 ~ 0 (mm)

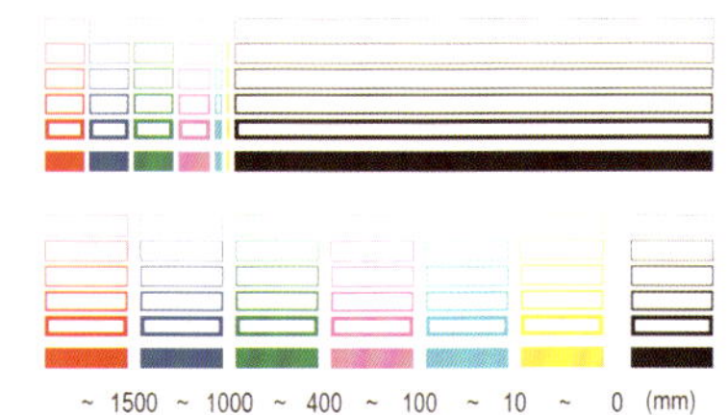

4.15 Building Masquerade 2.

Diagram of fake façade components.

scale : 1 / 150

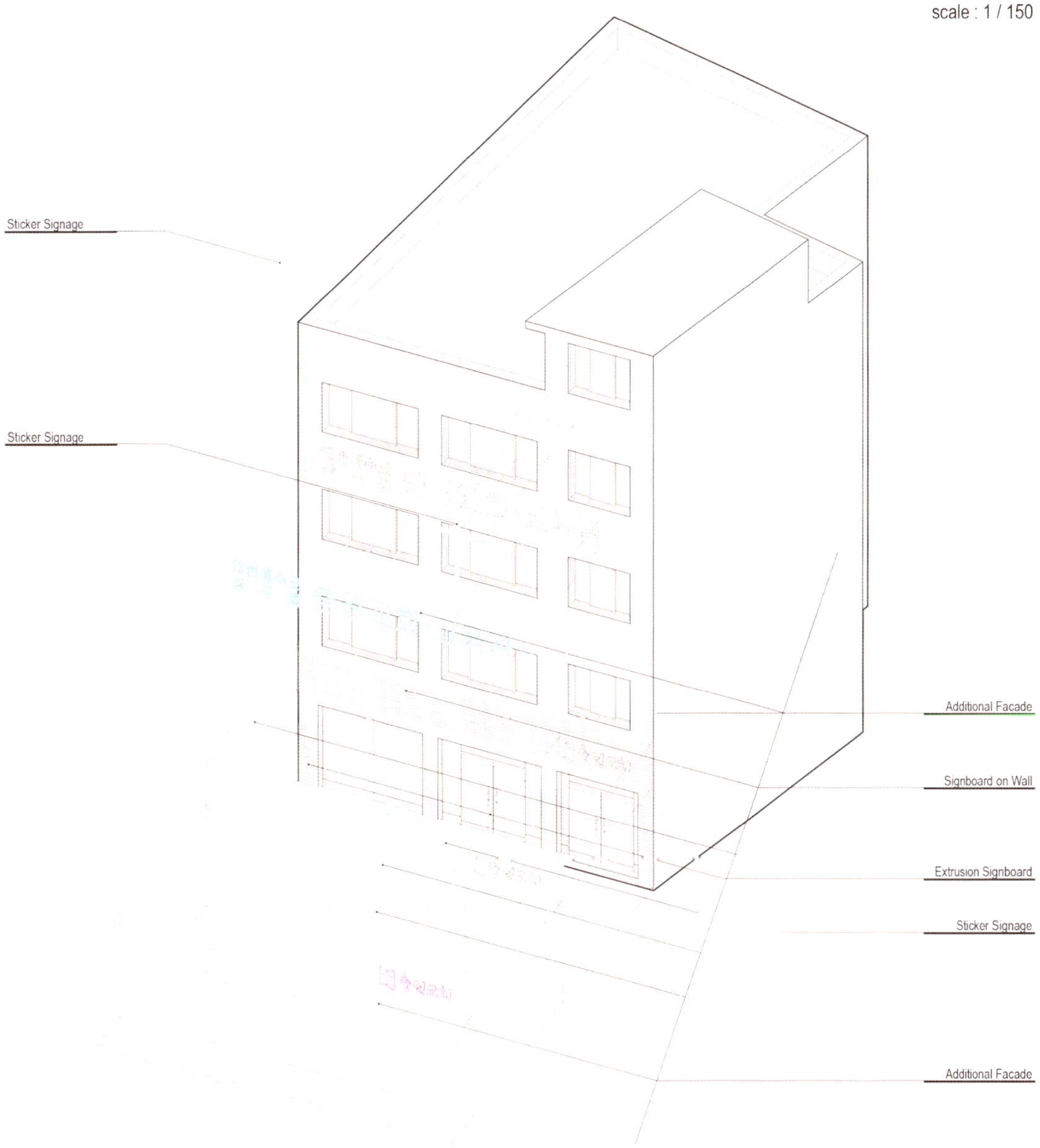

Sticker Signage
Sticker Signage
Additional Facade
Signboard on Wall
Extrusion Signboard
Sticker Signage
Additional Facade

Building Height : 18.4m
Building Storeys: 6 / 1 (Above Ground / Underground)
Commercial Usage : 5 / 1
Area :

Appraised Value of Land : About $19,333/㎡ (2019)

~ 1500 ~ 1000 ~ 400 ~ 100 ~ 10 ~ 0 (mm)

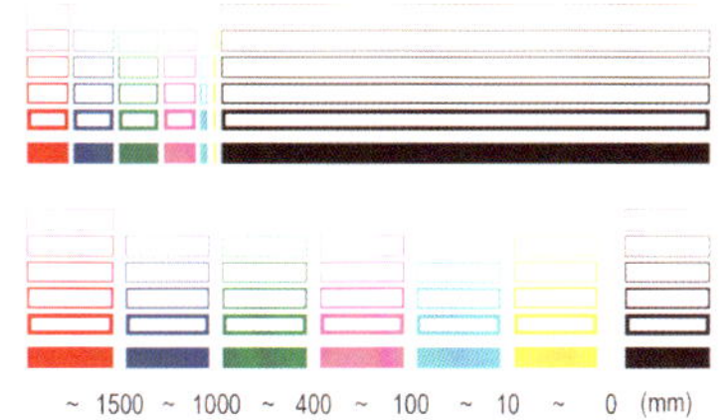

<u>4.16 Vertical Urban Factory.</u>

Adaptive reuse project drawings.

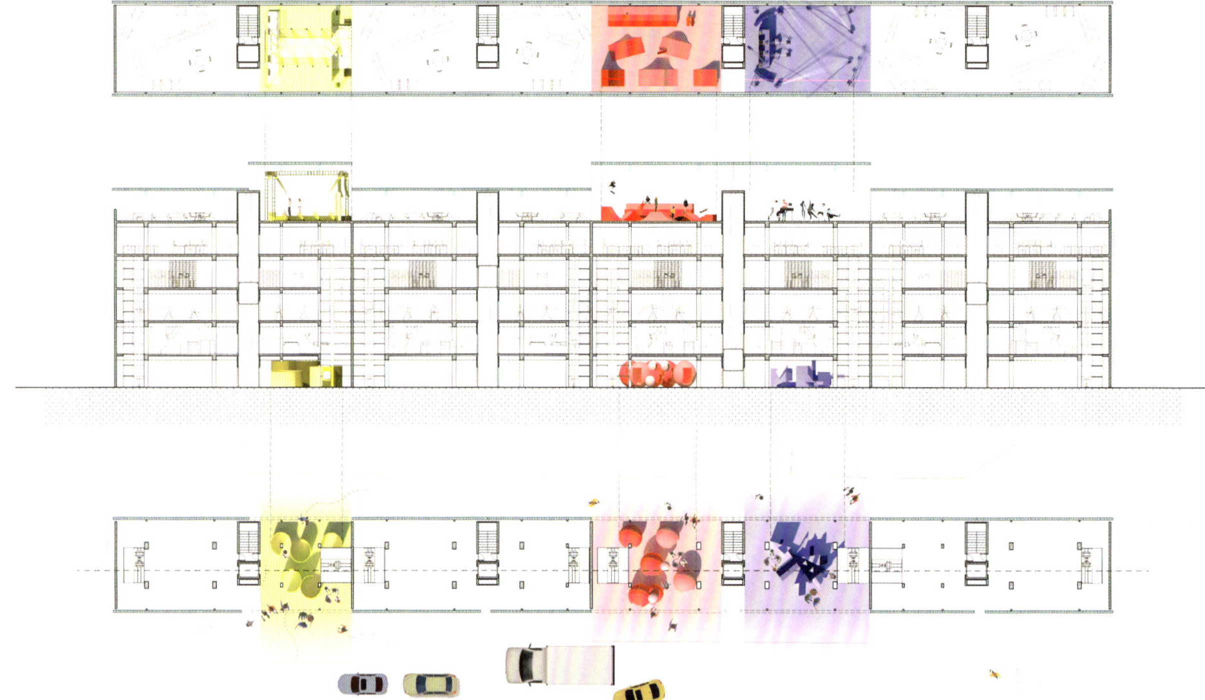

façade is a possibility. For example, a 100-metre long building that runs parallel to the Cheonggyecheon stream in the central business district of Seoul was retrofitted with movable façades to house vertical factories. [4.16 and 4.17]. Because of its length, the building is sectioned vertically as rowhouses where startup micro-production companies can run research, design, and sales for a designated period. The façade covers the entire micro-factory while in production, and it opens up to produce a pop-up market at ground level and there is an event space on the roof for promotions. The purpose is to create a dynamic, ever-changing streetscape. The facilities can run as a city-sponsored program for entrepreneurs, incentivising local circular economies.

4.17 Vertical Factory.

Model of transformable façade.

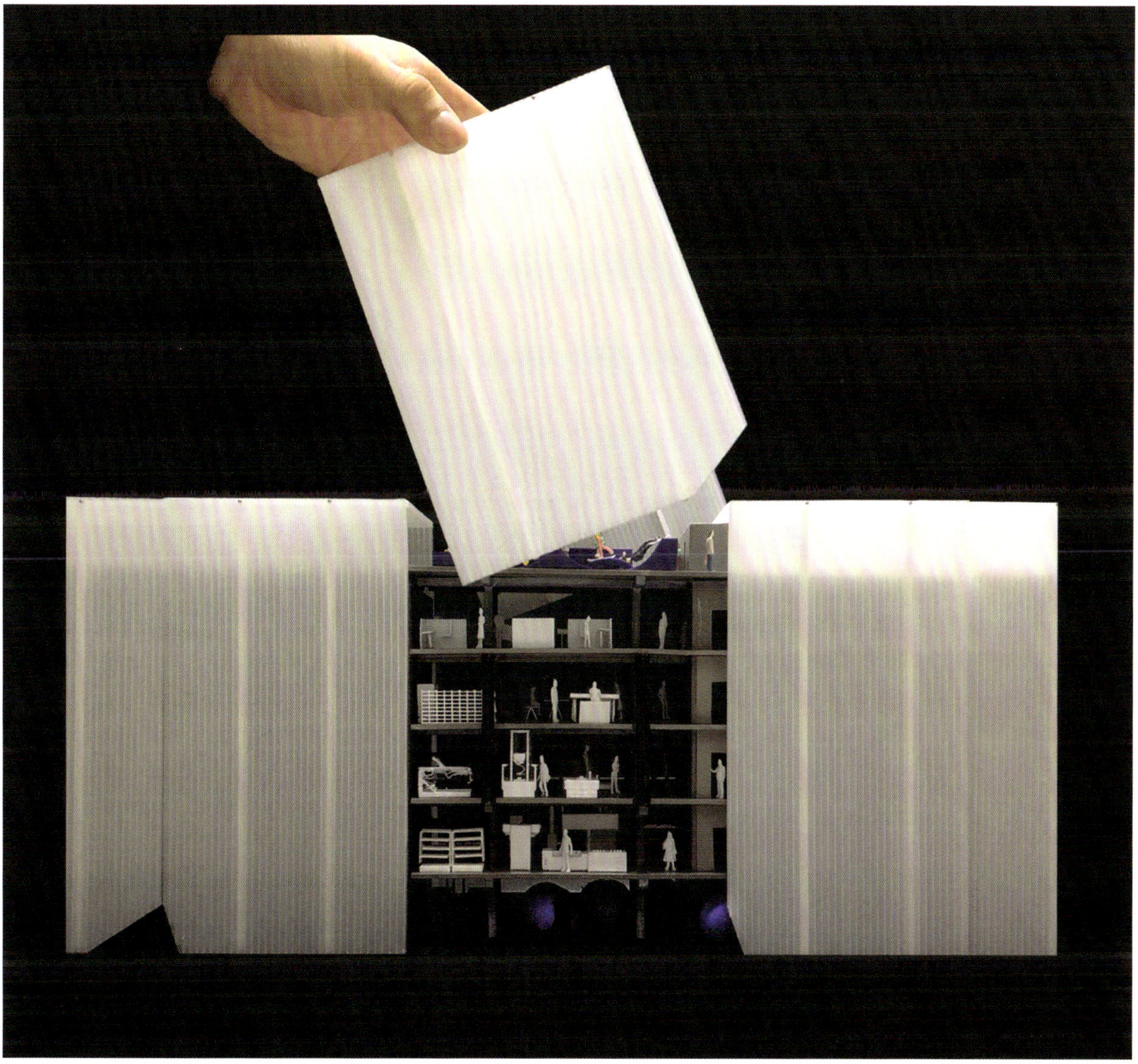

Semiotic Elements

Architectural shells could perhaps be conceptualised as urban stage backdrops, disassociated from the interior programing and façade signs.

The Duck and Decorated Shed[18] famously established the polemic between sign and symbol in architecture. Should the form of a building signify anything, or should a sign do the work of indicating a building's use? Form, by itself, can convey a meaning—for example, the configuration of hand gestures produces sign language. In the context of Seoul's commercial density, buildings get inundated with signs that take over entire façades. [4.18]. The signs are not intended to be part of the architecture, yet they define the image of the building. Architecture becomes lost behind these semiotic elements that represent distributed portions of the whole. Environments of hyperactivity work with an architecture that serves as background scaffolding, unless the sign itself becomes the system for space making.

The semiotic element was also found as a symbolic form that could be attached to any structure, changing its program. The cross turret on top of a building announces that there is a church inside that building, which also holds a restaurant as announced by a sign. The sign as text and sign as form cohabitate within the same structure, which remains in the background and questions the value of the original architecture.

The installation in 4.22 and 4.23 demonstrates the use of commercial signs being used as a spatial system. There is no discrepancy between the original structure and its attachments as it is one and the other.

4.18 Sign Building.
Building corner covered with signs.

4.19 Cross Turret.

Diagram of cross attachment structure.

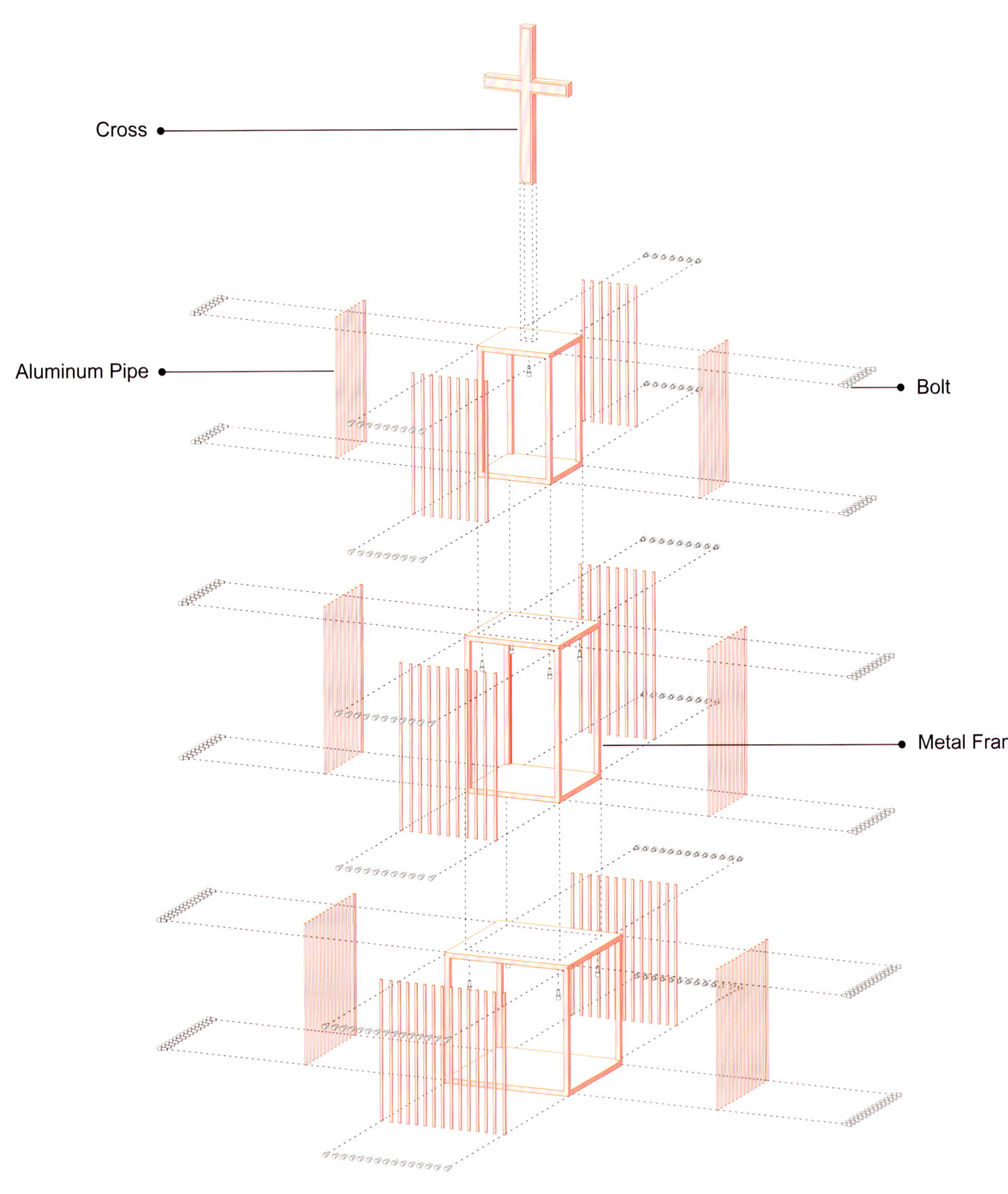

4.20 Instant Church.

Cross turret attached to existing building.

12mm Se
영재한의원
THEREWERY
영재한의원
123-4567
집삼겹살

4.21 Façade Sign.

Axon diagram of façade sign.

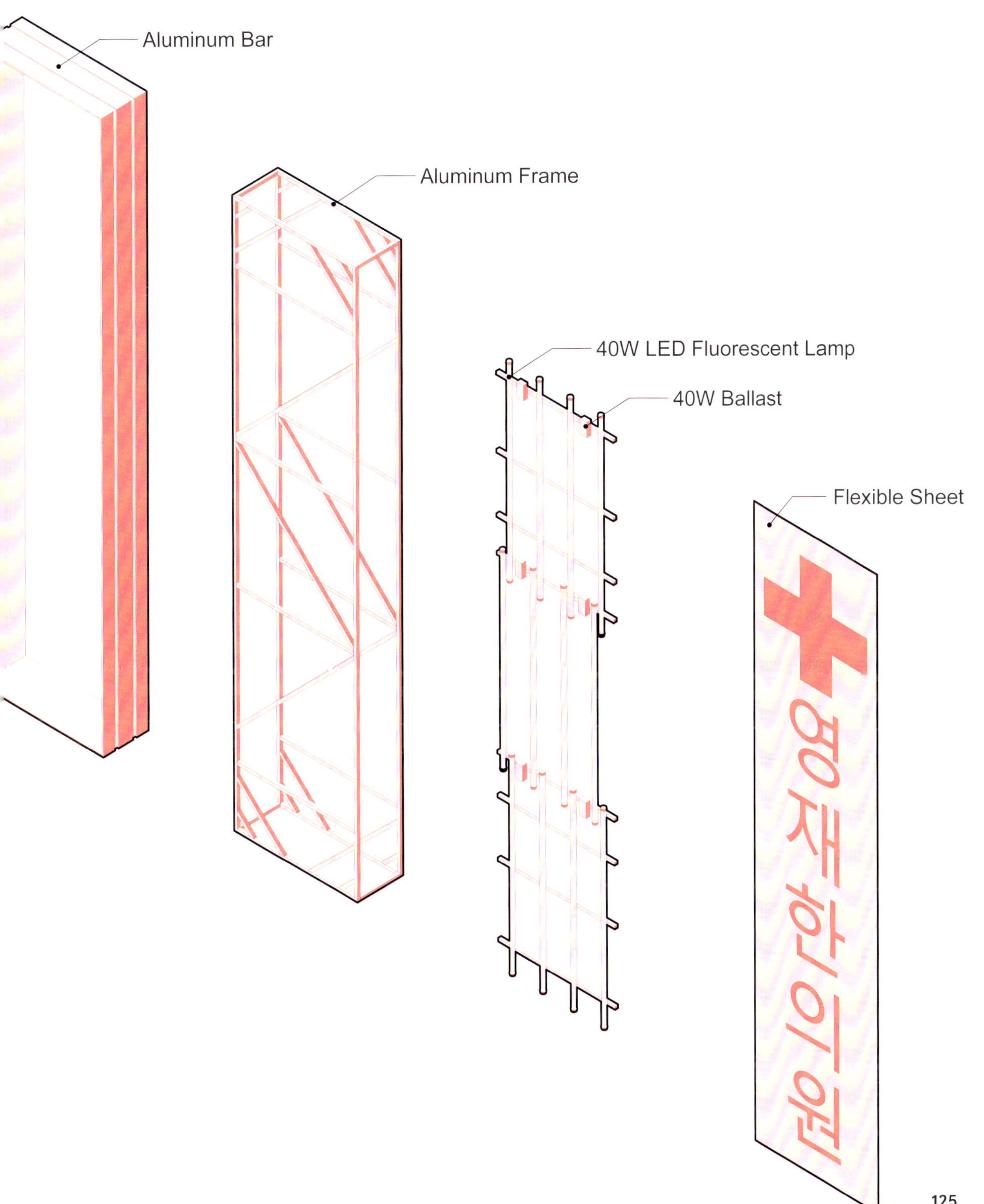

4.22 Sign Pavilion.

Photo of Installation (**Border Borderless**) of façade signs stacking as a spatial system.

4.23 Semantic Performative.

Close-up of the Sign Pavilion.

东方商店
1. 소매
TEL : 0415-214-6066
arui
生命之水富汽水
기적의 물 수소수의 발견
수소수 제조기 엘라임 186-0415-2195

Tai Yang
Shang Dian
태양상점 太阳商店
태양에네르기 발전계통 전문 생산 판매
A+ 고효율 정품 태양판 25년 담보
전화 : 0415-3885670

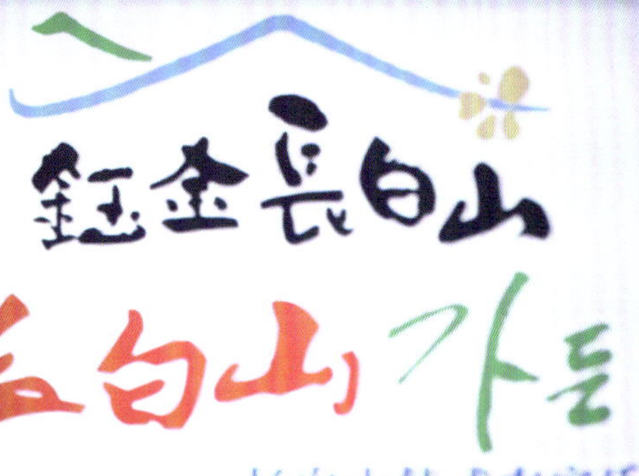

長白山
長白山 가든
长白山韩式农家乐
한식 韓式

Perfomative Elements

The lost space that exists for holding all the elements that allow buildings to perform can be described as Junkspace.[19]

"Junkspace seems an aberration, but it is essence, the main thing... product of the encounter between escalator and air conditioning, conceived in an incubator of sheetrock (all three missing from the history books). Continuity is the essence of Junkspace; it exploits any invention that enables expansion, deploys the infrastructure of seamlessness: escalator, air conditioning, sprinkler, fire shutter, hot-air curtain.... It is always interior, so extensive that you rarely perceive limits; it promotes disorientation by any means (mirror, polish, echo)....Junkspace is sealed, held together not by structure, but by skin, like a bubble ."[20]

Junkspace is the residue of modernising architecture, and is perhaps not conceived as architecture in itself. It is the subconscious part of buildings—the guts—that are organised mainly by other professionals and consultants, not the architect. In 2014, Koolhaas served as the director of the Venice Biennale, and selected the theme Fundamentals, with the main exhibition titled Elements of Architecture.

"Elements of Architecture looks under a microscope at the fundamentals of our buildings, used by any architect, anywhere, anytime: the floor, the wall, the ceiling, the roof, the door, the window, the façade, the balcony, the corridor, the fireplace, the toilet, the stair, the escalator, the elevator, the ramp."[21]

The overall exhibition revisited the evolution of the elements quoted before, yet the entrance to the exhibition was an installation of a mechanical space, hung from the rafters and covered by a drop ceiling. This specific installation at the entrance of the pavilion demonstrated a proportional value of almost half and half between the junkspace and the usable space in architecture. Without listing all these vents and systems as part of the collection of elements, the installation made it evident that, perhaps, they need to be reconsidered as these elements help define the performance of a space in terms of its habitability.

4.24 Junkspace.

Entry to the Elements exhibition at the 2014 Venice Biennale.

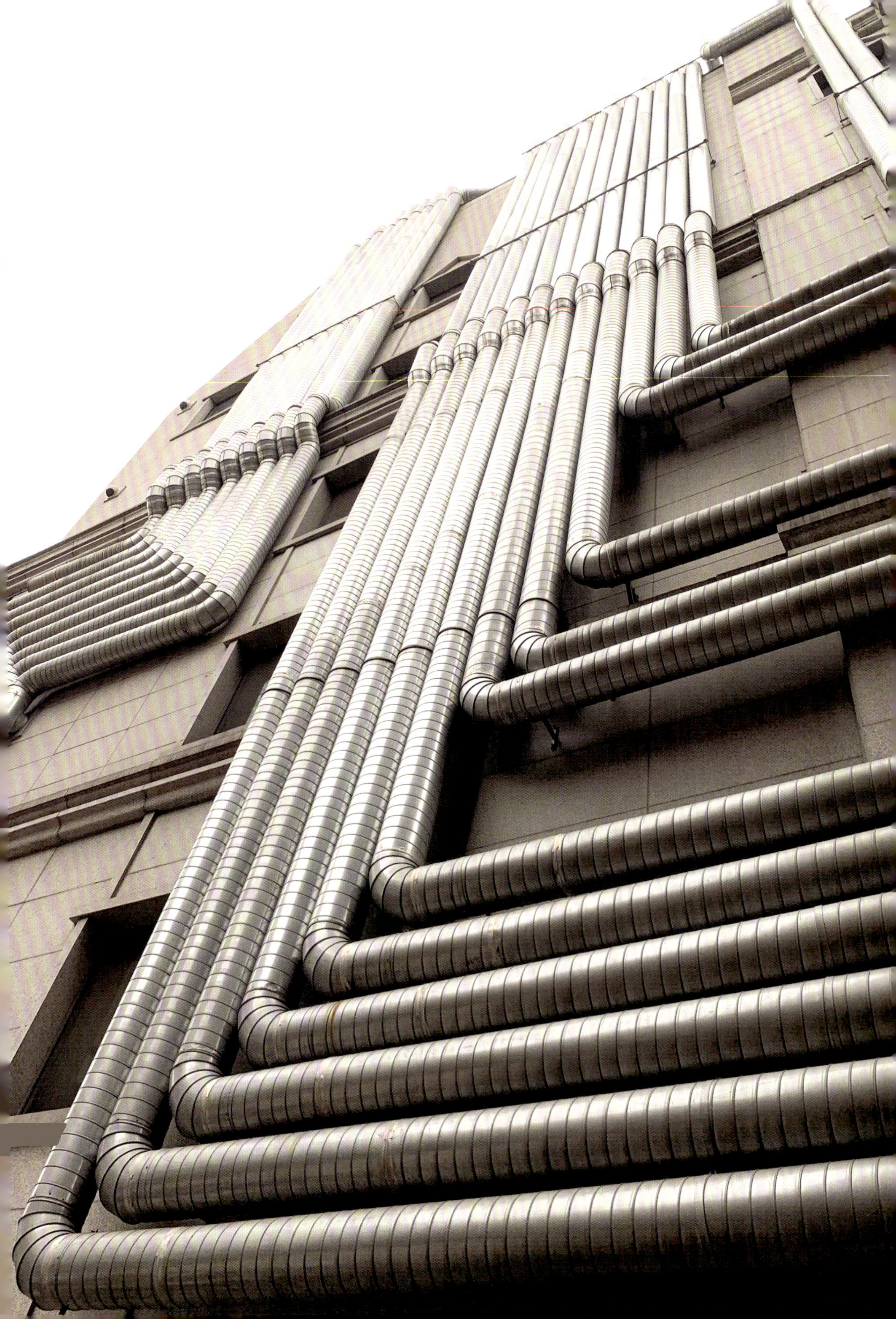

4.25 Perfomative Ornamental.

Exhaust vents attached to a façade in an orderly pattern.

4.26 Vented Adapative Reuse.

Exhaust vents attached to a facade based on allowable insertions.

The high-tech architecture of the 1970s addressed this condition by exposing mechanical elements on façades, giving the interior space more flexibility of use with an unobstructed universal space. If the goal is to achieve more dynamic, flexible, and equitable environments, the concept of an unobstructed universal space should be prioritised.

In Seongsu, production facilities expose mechanical elements in their true form on the exterior of the building as attachments. These are not fashioned after the high-tech architects, but done after the fact, as accessories for adapting and reusing existing buildings. They optimise the use of modern slab buildings allowing them to perform as factories. Some are arranged in an orderly fashion, taking an ornamental role, while others are installed as needed over time and have no formal arrangement.

Productive Elements counteract the rigid zoning regulations offering variability and adaptability.

In an East Asian context, it is common to replace older buildings with new ones after a 30-year period in a tabula rasa process. In Seoul, entire blocks are demolished in order to make way for new construction that offers higher density, housing blocks being the most common. This approach has the effect of producing monocultural urban islands. Apartment blocks are typically developed in this manner, combining multiple parcels into a singular parcel to form a block. Construction companies can then develop thousands of households as a singular project, under one brand. The images in 4.27 and 4.28 illustrate this process in two dynamic neighbourhoods: Euljiro and Seongsu.

Both neighbourhoods have a diversity of programs within a fine-grained, low-rise urban fabric that allows communities to thrive. Micro-industries can also be found here, producing circular economies. With the replacement of these neighbourhoods for apartment blocks, there is a loss of diversity that may not only be a problem of displacing present communities, but also may be contradictory to the future demographics of Seoul. With Seoul's aging and declining population, it might be more sustainable to retrofit the existing urban fabric, rather than keep building new. As the demographics in Seoul start dramatically changing, the discrepancy between the density of buildings and the density of population might cause urban voids. As an adaptive reuse strategy, focusing on elements might provide the most flexibility for retrofitting buildings into diverse multifunctional environments. Figure 4.29 and Figure 4.30 depict how, through the implementation of elements, a whole neighbourhood can change while maintaining the existing architectural background. Yet, this condition raises polemics regarding its implementation in the real world. Within the context of de-zoning the city as a way to alleviate the problems caused by modernist planning, the implementation of productive elements might still need to be restricted to certain areas, but instead of functional zoning, this can happen within typological blocks. This phenomenon is currently occurring within a low-rise, high-density urban

4.27 Euljiro Block Development.

Sequence of demolition of small structures to combine into a single block in Euljiro.

4.28 Seongsu Block Development.

Sequence of demolition of small structures to combine into a single block in Seongsu.

4.29 Diagrams of a street façade.

Before and after the attachment of elements.

4.30 Diagrams of a streetscape.

Before and after the attachment of elements.

4.31 Urban Maison Domino System

Photo of modern building as a pure system.

fabric with the majority of buildings being villa types of about four storeys. This typology allows for the appropriation of the elements to produce a mizing over the architectural backdrop. This might not be the same case in a high-rise apartment block. Seoul already has distinctive typological blocks[22] that would allow for this phenomenon to be repeated or tested in a controlled manner through clusters. This approach would allow for a diversity of experiences within the city, as well as free range to experiment with production and elements in certain typological blocks that could be distributed throughout the city.

So far, we have distinguished between spatial, semiotic, ornamental, and performative categories of elements that serve specific roles. These elements can be used independently to transform a single-use building into an urban microcosm. The photo collage in 4.32 demonstrates how very simple operations of injecting ready-made elements into an existing framework can mutate the environment. The scene depicted in the collage could be easily found as a real condition in Seoul.

The element as a plug-in solution questions the role of architecture as a finalised piece of work or an initial framework for which to organically grow, as needed. The notion of rethinking architecture from the point of view of the element would require a reconsideration of the roles of an element in itself. Should it be regulated and standardised as a designed element, or should it remain as a borrowed form. If the element is regulated and standardised, then city would lose a sense of spontaneity. This is common in cities in Europe, for example, where signs, fences, and street lights are standardised to produce a cohesive image of the city. This is not the case for a city of Seoul, where the variety of elements produce a dynamic streetscape. If the elements are to be thought of as designed, they can also be cross-categorised in order to perform multiple roles, and create new elements. For example, the Sign Pavilion Installation in 4.22 sought to use a semiotic element in a spatial role, becoming a system. The transformable façade in the vertical factory project allowed for the whole space to expand, serving both an ornamental and spatial role. The vents on the façade are performative and ornamental, when properly arranged. This merger of roles creates the productive element as a new category for multiplicity and diversity within a single piece of architecture that can lead to a more sustainable, resilient, and equitable urbanity.

4.32 Urban Microcosm

Collage of modern building after the attachment of elements.

4.33 Elements Project.

Shows all the borrowed elements have been left in their original industrial form, and have been coloured red for standardisation. By making all the elements the same colour, they become part of the spatial system of interchangeable parts that produce an architectural effect.

Endnotes

1 United Nations Habitat for a Better Future. 2020. World Urban Forum 10 (WUF10).

2 Moreno, Carlos. 2022. "Paris Ville Du Quart D'heure, Ou Le Pari De La Proximité." Paris Ville Du Quart D'heure, Ou Le Pari De La. https://www.paris.fr/dossiers/paris-ville-du-quart-d-heure-ou-le-pari-de-la-proximite-37.

3 Ajuntament de Barcelona. 2022. "Supermanzana Barcelona: Nueva Etapa." Barcelona, Ajuntament De Barcelona. https://ajuntament.barcelona.cat/superilles/es/.

4 Seoul Metropolitan Government. 2022. "The Sharing City Seoul Project." Official Website of the Seoul Metropolitan Government. https://english.seoul.go.kr/policy/key-policies/city-initiatives/1-sharing-city/.

5 ARK Investment Management LLC. "Geopolitics, Innovation, and Deglobalization with Peter Zeihan." YouTube, May 21, 2022, https://youtu.be/t_gw4eTr-hM.

6 KOSIS. "Projected Population by Age (Province)." Kosis, 2022. https://kosis.kr/statHtml/statHtml.do?orgId=101&tblId=DT_1BPB001&vw_cd=MT_ETITLE&list_id=A41_30&scrId=&language=en&seqNo=&lang_mode=en&obj_var_id=&itm_id=&conn_path=MT_ETITLE&path=%252Feng%252FstatisticsList%252FstatisticsListIndex.do.

7 Ibid.

8 Jung, Inha. Architecture and Urbanism in Modern Korea. Honolulu: University of Hawaii Press, 2014, 53.

9 Ibid.

10. The Seoul Research Data Service. "Industries in Seoul." Industries in Seoul, 2011. https://data.si.re.kr/data/%ED%86%B5%EA%B3%84%EB%A1%9C-%EB%B3%B8-%EC%84%9C%EC%9A%B8-%EC%98%81%EB%AC%B8%ED%8C%90/329.

11. Ibid.

12. Seoul Solution. "The Social Maps of Seoul." Seoul Solution, August, 30, 2021. https://www.seoulsolution.kr/en/content/3324.

13. Kim, Sun-Wung. "Urban Planning System of Seoul." Seoul Solution, October 9, 2017. https://www.seoulsolution.kr/en/node/6310.

14. Laugier, Marc-Antoine, et al. An Essay on Architecture. Los Angeles, California: Hennessey & Ingalls, 2009.

15. Ibid. P.13

16. Durand, Jean-Nicolas-Louis. Précis Of the Lectures on Architecture. Los Angeles, California: Getty Research Institute, 2000.

17. Moussavi, Farshid, and Michael Kubo. The Function of Ornament. Barcelona: Actar, 2008.

18. Venturi, Robert, et al. Learning from Las Vegas. Cambridge, Massachusetts: The MIT Press, 2017.

19. Koolhaas, Rem. Junkspace. October, Vol. 100, 2002, 175–190. https://doi.org/10.1162/016228702320218457.

20. Ibid.

21. Koolhaas, Rem. "Biennale Architettura 2014 2014: Elements of Architecture." La Biennale Di Venezia, November 28, 2017. https://www.labiennale.org/en/architecture/2014/elements-architecture.

22. Luna, Rafael. "Insular Structures, The Megalopolis of Seoul: Analyzing Urban Mutations Based on the City's Typological Subunits." Topos, vol. 113, 2020, 76–81.

Dialogue with Tali Hatuka: The Productive Element

This chapter is the transcript of a discussion between the architecture firm PRAUD (Rafael Luna and Dongwoo Yim) and Tali Hatuka, Professor of Urban Design and Planning at Tel Aviv University. Tali joined the discussion via zoom from Tel Aviv, and PRAUD met with the other contributors on 16 November 2022 at Domansa in Seoul to discuss the topic of the productive element. The discussion dealt with issues of zoning and regulations for façade attachments that appear in neighbourhoods like Seongsu in Seoul. Industrial elements, such as vents and ducts, are attached to the exterior of buildings as additional items, transforming banal buildings into urban factories. These elements are not part of the original building, nor are they designed in an ornamental manner. They are functional in nature for the purpose of increasing the performance of the building based on its new industrial program in the middle of a mixed-use neighborhood. While these productive elements are not architectural in their nature, PRAUD proposes that the architectural element needs to be re-evaluated to include borrowed elements from other fields, generating a debate for their distribution to remain as an ad-hoc phenomenon or as regulated designed items to maintain a designed aesthetic for the urban streetscapes.

Rafael Luna:
For a bit of background on the precinct project, we are looking at the transition cities are making in relation to resiliency, policy making, and sustainability. We have seen a rise in projects such as the 15-Minute City in Paris, the Supermanzana in Barcelona, and the Sharing City in Seoul. These projects touch on resiliency, sustainability, and equity and have become even more relevant after experiencing disruption in the global supply chain during the COVID-19 disease pandemic, along with the Suez Canal blockage. These were unexpected events that we could not have prepared for and have disruptive consequences. These unforeseen events are commonly referred to as black swan events, and more recently they have strengthened the thinking around the need for more localised supply chains, and how to live, entertain, consume, and produce within our own precincts. The precinct project is looking at how architecture can become a tool for addressing these issues, with an emphasis on the elements of architecture. Theoretically, we can discuss the role of the element as spatial, ornamental, semiotic, and performative. Yet, in Seoul, we see the implementation of the borrowed industrial element as an attachment that transforms banal buildings into urban centres of production. We see the appropriation of buildings as micro-cities, filled with multiple programs that the users have appropriated by attaching these elements. This phenomenon achieves the goal of providing accessibility to services and amenities without being so invasive. It reinstates the idea of adaptive reuse as a sustainable approach through these micro-incisions using the idea of the element. Tali, you come from a planning background, and one of the issues that has been raised is how these architectural provocations relate to zoning laws and regulations. Can you offer a different point of view from just seeing this as an architectural phenomenon?

Tali Hatuka:
Firstly, thank you for inviting me to this discussion. I am also an architect, but in the past decade I have been working more on urban design and planning. Developing a language of elements is a great idea to consider the flexibility of buildings. I do not see it as provocative though; I see it as a rational idea where you can expand the elements that you have identified and add new ones. There are three issues to think about: first, is this system of elements flexible? Second, do these elements form a "language"? And third, if yes, how do these elements create sentences? These raise other questions as well. Is the language created through self-organisation by the user, or managed by architects? Say if I have a building, who adapts the elements to turn the building into a factory?

Rafael Luna:
If you have free zoning to do whatever you want, then it might rely on the tenant.

Tali Hatuka:
But are these elements arranged through the self-organisation, or designed by experts?

Dongwoo Yim:
In the semi-industrial zone of Seongsu, I think it is more a self-evolving phenomenon. Because the zone is in the middle of the city, it cannot accommodate a huge factory. The urban fabric is tight in this neighbourhood, but industries still need to exist and produce here. The existing architecture is very generic, not necessarily factory typologies. Depending on the type of production, tenants will have different needs for how they use the existing buildings. For example, industries with heavy machinery might need a stable supply of electricity, so they will attach their own power generators, so their machines never lose power. In the same building, you might have another industry that produces a lot of fumes, and they will attach vent ducts to exhaust the fumes. So, the appropriations from the industries create a self-evolving factory typology through these attachments.

Another phenomenon that is occurring here in Seongsu is the loss of capital power in some industries. Therefore, some buildings are transformed into commercial or cultural spaces, and the production elements are removed, while the architecture remains. So it is primarily the tenant who plays with these elements, especially since the elements are seen as temporal, and do not have strict regulations from the city.

Tali Hatuka:
So, you have a couple of options here. One is understanding this informal development and its logic, and keeping it informal. The other is to formalise the development and create a system, a language, supported by regulations, while trying to keep this system flexible. If it is informal, then perhaps it is a planning issue. Is it restricted to a particular area? What we have seen in our studies from various cities around the world is that these neighbourhoods are very dynamic, but they also create a lot of issues in terms of environmental performance. Do you want to restrict this dynamic to a particular area in the city? Right now, we are discussing the concept in a very abstract way. But is it only happening in a specific district in Seoul and, if so, what are the boundaries of that district? And is it going to be formalised because, if not, then regulation is not an issue. From my perspective, I would say it needs to be a flexible language, monitored by regulations, while allowing flexibility for tenants. It is an interesting idea, but you are working with elements that currently exist. Perhaps there are new elements that would justify regulation. Elements by themselves are not a language. For example, do buildings of one storey and buildings of five storeys use the same elements? Should their use of elements be controlled, or should they be offered options? How should designers work with this taxonomy? For me, playing with the elements is the key to thinking about cities. Right now, there are the elements and there are the buildings. To talk about a city, you need to understand how the elements are interacting and whether or

not you want to introduce new elements that somehow also take care of the environment.

Dongwoo Yim:
Do you think writing guidelines would be useful?

Tali Hatuka:
I think what we are talking about is synchronic typologies, where you have different uses within the same building. The question is, should these synchronic typologies be spread throughout the city or condensed to a particular place? Do you develop guidelines that address aesthetics, environmental issues, performance, flexibility, and time? It is a very complex issue that I am not sure should be left up to the market or the tenant. But we also do not want to overregulate, so it is a very delicate interplay. For me, the elements present a starting point. They are a great opportunity for adaptive, resilient cities. However, the language of the elements is still not clear nor developed enough to discuss within urban design or planning, as yet. As an urban designer and planner, I would say you need to create a system for thinking about typologies and guidelines. Culture also plays a major role and the different scale of buildings will imply different sets of elements. It would be interesting to see different typologies of buildings and their association to the elements in different districts.

Graham Crist:
I am fascinated by the tension it throws up. I am reading PRAUD's part of the project as taking all those elements that sit outside architectural design and bringing them into a compositional field, celebrating that they are unregulated. The question is, would that energy be destroyed once the elements are systemised or highly regulated? It makes me think about other conditions, such as the appropriation of rooftops for example, that do not fall under permits but fall into a grey zone for regulations.

John Doyle:
In Australia, as long as your building does not have a heritage listing, you can attach solar panels on it anywhere with no permit.

Silvia Micheli:
I would like to shift the discussion a bit, taking the idea of the elements from a post-modern point of view where we celebrate them as language. From surveying and recording the taxonomy and the manipulation necessary to create a syntax, I wonder how this project can become a tool to play with the elements and to enhance their application?

Tali Hatuka:
I also want to add another dimension to the discussion. The perspective so far has been from the building façades and their envelope; however, how the elements are experienced from within is also very important. It is something that needs to be addressed in order to be able to discuss syntax and will also influence how to think about urban design and planning. Again, I suggest that we think about the elements through different scale buildings and different typologies; but the next step is to play with the concepts much more.

Rafael Luna:
Right now, we have documented the phenomenon through direct observation. We see this as a starting point, but it has also raised a polemic in the topic moving forward. That is, if you design these elements, then it standardises the phenomenon and the city may appear more orderly, but perhaps more boring. What makes these neighbourhoods in Seoul exciting is the fact that they are created through appropriations with elements from other industries.

Tali Hatuka:
You do not have to standardise the relationship between the elements, but you can expand the taxonomy of elements. You can offer different kind of elements—something new without been strict and rigid.

Dongwoo Yim:
We started this research on the productive element by walking around, observing, and marking what is happening in the neighbourhood. The reason this neighbourhood is so dynamic and flexible is because of the small elements, and not

because of the buildings. As architects, we asked, what's our role? Do we just need to design a box and let the tenants decide what they want to do that box? Perhaps this is the most flexible way to use the city.

Graham Crist:
If you consider the box as an armature for all these elements, then you can exaggerate the role much more, asking the designer to account for it much more actively.

Rafael Luna:
Architecture in that sense should be seen as a scaffolding.

Dongwoo Yim:
Or platform.

Graham Crist:
Or a reflection of capitalism.

John Doyle:
The scaffolding does not have to be simple. If you take the view that architecture is not just problem solving, or about finding the optimum form, then there is an opportunity to make a scaffolding that problematises relationships with the elements or rather exaggerates them. We see the city formed by simple boxes where the attachment of the elements makes them exciting, but perhaps if we talk about the future of the practice, it might be the design of the scaffolding that has a dynamic relationship with the elements rather than a mute canvas, or, alternatively, the elements could be the medium of servicing buildings when they need to be adapted. And as we design in that space, we use the interstitial space as the only space in architecture where we can exercise innovation. We talk about complete randomness or systematisation, but in the middle is design, which is neither. Perhaps the potential is that instead of fully codifying the element as a regulation or completely ignoring it, where it is partially regulated or ignored, design is what mediates the impact of these elements in the city. We can create elements that contribute to public benefit.

Silvia Micheli:
We were talking about what unites all these projects throughout the book and where we converge with our different scales. We have the same problem in our house project—we are tackling the boundaries of properties and trying to create a language and system there, but we have the same dilemma in that we do not want to design everything to the point that we lose the spontaneity of the process. And I expect that at the territorial level, you have the same elements and the same reasoning behind it, but at a much larger scale. Design is the key to responding to that. How do we reinvent these elements and how can we enhance the possibilities of using them and enhancing them?

Peyman Akhgar:
I think another important thing to consider is the democracy of space, which is important in designing domestic spaces, in particular. If you see what people want, then you can come up with the rules and regulations based on those wants, which is extremely democratic. However, if you are a planner, the rules and regulations are very controlled. Something I appreciate is that this system is a reflection of how people want to use the space. As people start using space, it becomes dynamic and democratic. In Australia, the use of space is highly regulated; but this system we are discussing seems to bend the rules and creates a completely different public space. Perhaps Australian cities can learn from this Korean phenomenon and then come up with planning and regulation strategies to fit this model.

Tali Hatuka:
Each industrial revolution dramatically changed the type of production and technology we use. We have to bear in mind that these ideas might not be relevant in 20 years. From a historical perspective, we are in the fourth industrial revolution now, and it might only work for 20 years. So this system needs to be flexible and dynamic. Production overloads infrastructure, so we cannot let anyone just open

a production space wherever they want. Therefore, it becomes a planning question. That is why this project of elements has several scales. Firstly, the elements and the possibility of expanding the taxonomy and relationship between elements. Secondly, the object itself, thinking about the elements from within the building. Thirdly, from an urban design perspective, you must develop guidelines that allow the flexibility of the system. When it comes to planning, zoning regulation is still needed because you want to take this language into account within the context of infrastructure; however, it might be that we want to have areas in the city that are not included in this type of development. People might choose to live in this type of hybrid environment, but others might not. So, the fourth scale is to ask is what is the city offering and what do different districts offer. Zoning is also a part of the environment and the type of production that is occurring. The project touches on these four scales with crucial questions—from the micro to the macro—which makes it an interesting project.

John Doyle:
That is an interesting point about infrastructure. One of the characteristics of Seongsu is the local nature of production and its manufacturing ecology, with little forklifts running up and down the streets. There is an intimate scale to this neighbourhood where commercial, residential, manufacturing, and production spaces work with each other. There is output and input, but not at a huge scale. The question of scale and proximity is very important. If these buildings were to increase their productive capacity, then would the neighbourhood remain intimate, or would it put a burden on the infrastructure, or could we imagine a future where this production capacity is distributed throughout the city?

Tali Hatuka:
We could look at all these scales through the lens of infrastructure. While I started with the question of formal versus informal production, now I do not think it is as relevant. A better way to think is through these different scales and across scales, understanding the complexity of this system. You can focus on the elements, the systems, and the infrastructure at varying scales. The system itself will help you to understand the formality and how, in 20 years, the next technological iteration of elements will work with these buildings. What we offer today will be temporal.

Graham Crist:
The division between formal and informal is correct; for example, if architects took the time to detail informal ductwork, then they dissolved that division entirely. An urban designer or planner does not care if the ductwork was put there by architects or not—it is just part of the fabric of the city. The question for the designer is, do they want to let go of that and let the city do its thing.

Rafael Luna:
One term we have been using in Seoul is de-zoning, but perhaps is not a matter of getting rid of zoning all together. If we talk about documenting the phenomena that we are seeing, it is not happening in apartment blocks. Perhaps the discussion is about conceptualising the typology of the blocks where the cluster of buildings allow for these appropriations to occur. This can account for market participants—be it developers looking to construct a high-rise or apartment block, or those looking to create productive blocks.

Tali Hatuka:
I think that the idea of clustering is important and thinking about the city in a more complex way. These phenomena of creating spaces of production through the elements cannot happen everywhere because it would be challenging for residents and because the typology of buildings are not the same. Restricting the phenomena to particular areas is quite important because development will be different in city centres than on the edge of the cities.

Rafael Luna:
Seongsu is already operating as a semi-industrial cluster, so in the matter of zoning and de-zoning, maybe it is about typological clusters.

Graham Crist:
It also raises the question about the performance of production. Zoning is a blank tool for relocating manufacturing because it might cause a nuisance. For example, I have a brewery near my home, but the production is highly controlled to the point where residents would not even know a factory is in the area.

Silvia Micheli:
In Brisbane we are noticing a lot of residents choosing to bring production into their homes. Through design, we can accommodate these needs and reduce daily commutes, while maximising the use of the place. Welcoming the idea of accepting production in areas that were not originally intended as productive spaces could increase the mixing of uses, which is something cities are looking to achieve.

Rafael Luna:
And with that, we conclude our discussion. Thank you all for your time.

3
TERRITORY

(Melbourne)

Graham Crist
John Doyle

Growing Tight Food

A self-feeding city requires agriculture at urban density using high-intensity production techniques, and a reshaped diet. The benefits of such a city to our environment and to our health would be enormous and would also make that city more liveable.

Every city's footprint is shadowed by another much larger footprint—one that supports the city's consumption of goods. Land areas much larger than inhabited city boundaries exist to produce the things that the city consumes. The largest productive area is agricultural land, which feeds the city population. It is fruitless to think of dense cities without considering the production footprint encircling it. The agricultural production for a city is not as simple as considering fields growing food outside the city limits; agriculture involves a vast production network, extending globally and co-opting industry, transport and farmlands far beyond the city limits. These elements of production translate to a footprint barely visible at the urban centre, but most extreme in effect where the city is very dense and affluent where high goods consumption contrasts with low consumption of inhabited land.

These effects became visible when we considered the benefits of very dense cities through our use of the term *supertight*.[1] For example, observing Manhattan's physical map overlaid on the huge ring representing its carbon footprint dismantles the notion that tighter urban structures are less consumptive of resources. We can also observe examples of large agricultural production areas across the Singaporean — Malaysian border to see urban outsourcing for a city-state importing nearly all of its food. [5.1].

5.1 Consumption Density vs Production Density.

The dense urban environment of Singapore is supported from a vast hinterland of agricultural production across the strait in Malaysia.

Terms like *food security* and *food miles* are now prevalent, with sprawling urban peripheries eating productive land. Many big cities import over 90 percent of their food from outside their national borders. They rely on international trade and long supply chains, on the climate of distant productive fields, and on transport that is mostly fossil fuel based. Even large national food producers transport great distances to their own cities, effectively competing with exporters. Calculating food miles and weighing them against other complex environmental factors underlies the huge carbon footprint of producing and distributing food. Global networks supersede regional and seasonal produce and support large-scale environmental modifications. Food miles and last miles focus the scale of the impact of food transport from international shipping to local supermarket car trips. These are design questions for productive cities. As cities expand at their low-density peripheries, they move into land once used for agriculture, while agricultural land replaces wilderness or forest.

Locating intensive farming within metropolitan areas for consumption within that city replaces imports from other agricultural areas. Could this strategy produce all the food for that city, making its boundary self-sufficient? This challenge is tested here under the specific metropolitan condition of Melbourne: a large city boundary and urban fabric hosting production, along with radical rethinking of agricultural techniques. There are numerous precedents for small market gardens producing commercial quantities of food; or micro-production in low-density community gardens. There is also an expanding field of experimentation with high-tech super-intense modes of agriculture, compatible with vertical repetition in dense urban areas.

We examined this proposition as a quantitative and qualitative, metropolitan-scale design question using greater Melbourne, Australia, as an urban food production testing site. Melbourne houses approximately five million people; it is highly affluent and growing quite rapidly with migration [2] [5.2]. It lies to the south of a rural food bowl producing significant amounts of exported agricultural produce. Metropolitan form and definition is crucial here. Consisting of 37 local administrative areas, Melbourne is also defined by an urban growth boundary created to curb sprawl into peripheral lands. Melbourne's dense central core joins a very large area of low-density suburbs and peri-urban or semi-rural land designated for future urban development. Its size makes metropolitan Melbourne well suited to interrogate urban agriculture.

5.2 Melbourne Sprawl.

Melbourne has an extremely low average density, with pockets of high density development.

5.3 Physical footprint vs productive footprint.

A comparison of the total land required to support cities overlaid on their actual physical footprint.

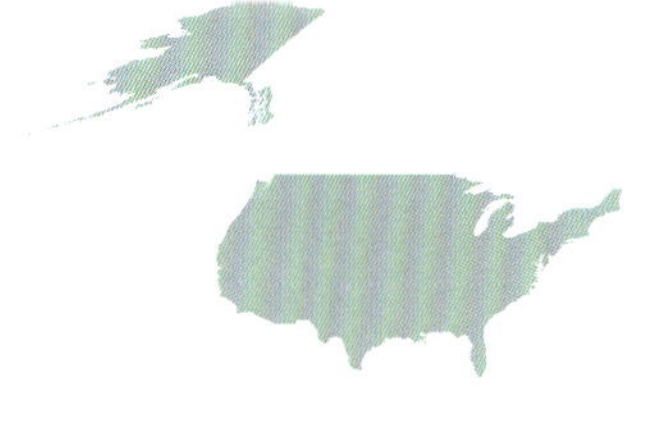

5.4 Feeding Hong Kong, China.

Global mapping of the countries providing the majority of Hong Kong, China's primary food supplies.

Urban Agricultural Net Zero

This design project asks: how much urban land can be made available for farming without losing city, and how much land is needed to feed an affluent metropolitan population?

Testing Melbourne's latent capacity to produce all of its consumed food began with establishing definitions and key metrics: population consumption demand; and productive land supply. Data from 2018 shows Melbourne's population at 4,936,003, increasing to 5,159,211 by mid 2020 with trends disrupted by the COVID-19 pandemic. We rounded this figure to five million.[3]

We then determined land requirements for agricultural production on a per capita basis. The Melbourne Foodprint Report provides food consumption and productive land use profile for the metropolis. The report breaks down current Melburnian consumption patterns according to food type. The data shows average Melbourne food consumption just over 1200 grams per capita per day.[4]

We multiplied the total consumption breakdown against the average land required to produce these food quantities.[5] This yielded estimates of total land requirements satisfying present metropolitan food consumption, as shown in 5.3. We thus estimated approximately 11,676,000 hectares in total is required based on average food consumption and category production statistics. Cross-referencing this figure against the Melbourne Foodprint Report estimating 16,300,000 hectares, and the Global Footprint Network estimating 8,748,902 hectares, this provides a reasonable baseline to compare future speculations, and to measure potential impacts of adopting high-density agricultural practices.

Determining available productive land asks: what would it take to produce Melbourne's annual food requirements within the city itself? Having determined total land areas required for food production, we estimated Melbourne's total available productive land.

Greater Melbourne land was defined within a 60-kilometre radius, being the maximum extent of the urban growth boundary.[6] This radius also means roughly one hour of travel time from the centre of the city to the edge. A circular zone with a 120-kilometre diameter centred on Melbourne's central business district and Port Phillip Bay was adopted as a project definition of Greater Melbourne.

Data mapped in this circle determined existing land use patterns and estimated available land for repurposing to agricultural production. This data consolidated land use databases from the Victorian Department of Environment, Land, Water, and Planning.[7] Existing land use categories determined whether they could be considered for conversion to agricultural production. There are significant amounts of existing agricultural land within the Greater Melbourne area. Much of the land surrounding Melbourne is very fertile and historically provided the city's fresh vegetables via market gardens. The notion of feeding Melbourne from its immediate vicinity is not novel. More recently, importing produce from further away became commonplace. This has coincided with the erosion of Melbourne's fertile food bowl, largely rezoned for residential development. For this project, all existing agricultural land is retained for agricultural use, protected against non-agricultural development, and intensified in production. All existing land for housing, commercial, educational, or civic development, and recreational use was retained and excluded from potential agricultural development. Parkland and natural reserves were also retained and excluded from development.

Some existing land use categories were identified as available for vertical and high-intensity agricultural production. In addition to land already zoned for agricultural production (pasture, cropping etc.) land currently used for agricultural processing (abattoirs, storage etc.) was identified and mapped. Other land designated as vacant or allocated for redevelopment (development sites, brownfield, disused mining) and other land uses that could be incorporated into agricultural production (windfarm, photovoltaic solar field zones etc.) were identified and mapped into a consolidated agricultural allocation. This aggregate of agricultural and re-adapted land yields approximately 58,100 hectares. This is approximately five percent of the calculated total land requirement, suggesting that at current consumption rates, land use with traditional agriculture could not supply Melbourne's total food consumption needs.[8]

Intensifying Production

Vertical and high-intensity farming techniques are necessary in any scenario of a city meeting its own food needs. Expanding global demand places arable land under increasing pressure. Emerging agricultural production technologies that increase crops yields while reducing the required land and resources to produce them are being intensely researched.[9] Techniques for high-density production are being expanded and becoming more commonplace, particularly as the demand for out-of-season produce increases. High-density vertical farming is far more efficient than traditional agriculture, using less land, water and usually fewer chemicals. When food is produced close to where it is consumed, there is also reduced land and energy required to process and transport it. The high-density factory farming of animals (dairy, eggs, meat), generates efficiencies and well-known ethical problems related not only to animal welfare, but also health and environmental concerns associated with feeding practices and disease. [10]

Vertical high-density agriculture represents a very small portion of agricultural production in Australia. So what if our food was produced at the highest possible density? Intense agricultural densities were examined through precedent factory farms, including commercial mass farming facilities and small-scale experimental or demonstration projects [5.13]. Working from the food categories described in the Melbourne Foodprint Report, a series of precedents were identified for each category. Each precedent was documented spatially as a piece of architecture or infrastructure. For each precedent, total annual production was assessed against the gross land/floor area (GFA) requirements to achieve it. A ratio of land:GFA per tonne of annual production was calculated [5.7].

Different foods have very different land/floor area requirements—even within vegetable categories there are varied production requirements. Tomatoes use five times the area of root vegetables for the same food calories.[11] Averages were determined between the various precedents mapped[12] and traditional agricultural yields were adopted for categories where no high-density food production approaches existed. The high-density growing techniques allowed reduction in overall land footprints required for food production.

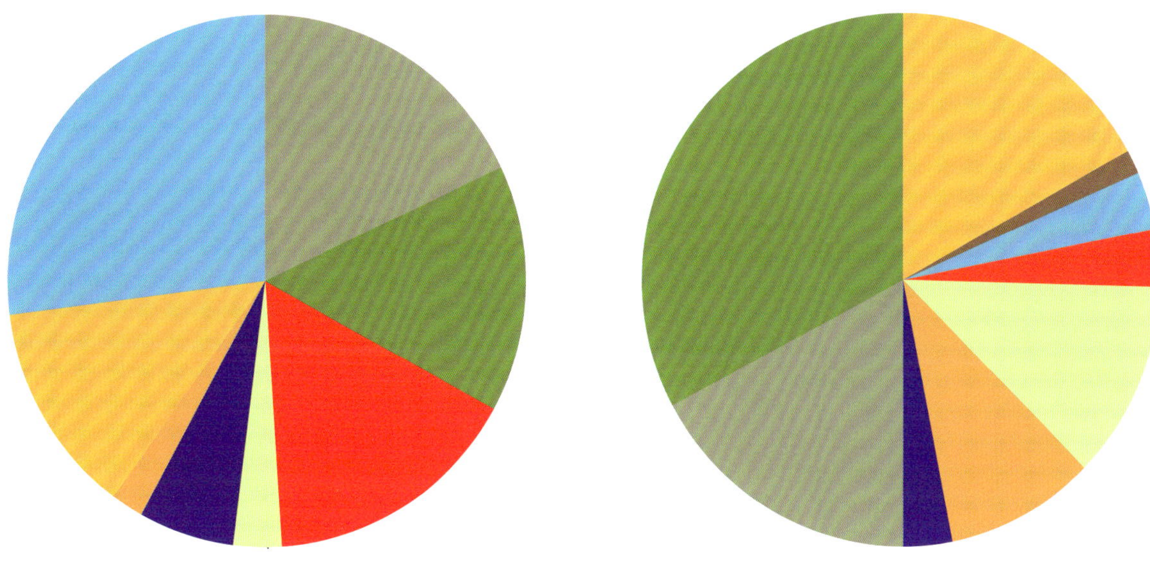

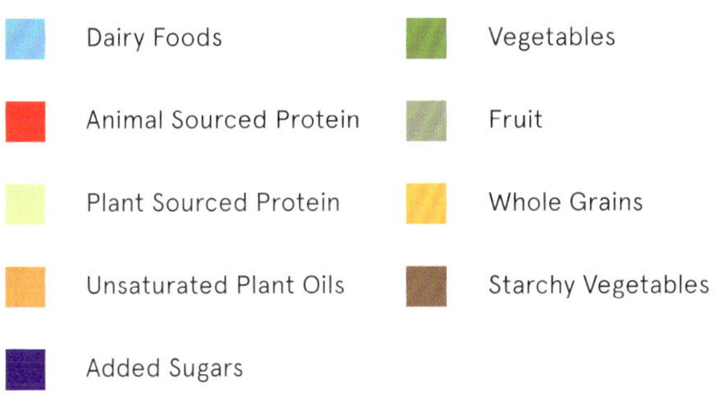

5.5 Designing Diet.

A comparison of the average Australian diet (left) with the EAT Lancet Healthy Reference diet (right).

5.6 Diet as a Planning Problem.

A comparison of the total footprint required (in land area of the state of Victoria) for the typical Australian Diet (left) vs the EAT Lancet Healthy Reference Diet (right).

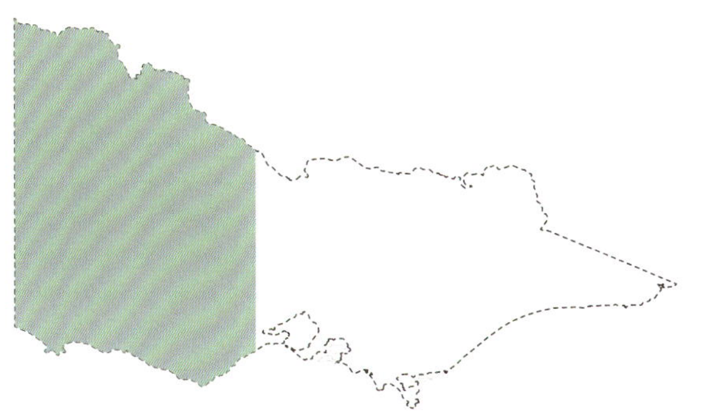

EGGS

VEGETABLES

FRUIT

SUGAR

RICE

CEREAL AND GRAINS

SEAFOOD

SALT

5.7 Agricultural Footprints.

The amount of land required to produce one tonne of different food types shown as comparable areas.

NUTS

LEGUMES

OILS

BEEF AND VEAL

CHICKEN

PORK

DAIRY

MUTTON AND LAMB

5.8 Growing Tight Melbourne.

GIS mapping of Metropolitan Melbourne's existing agricultural land, and brownfield land available for conversion to high density agricultural production within a 60 km radius of the city.

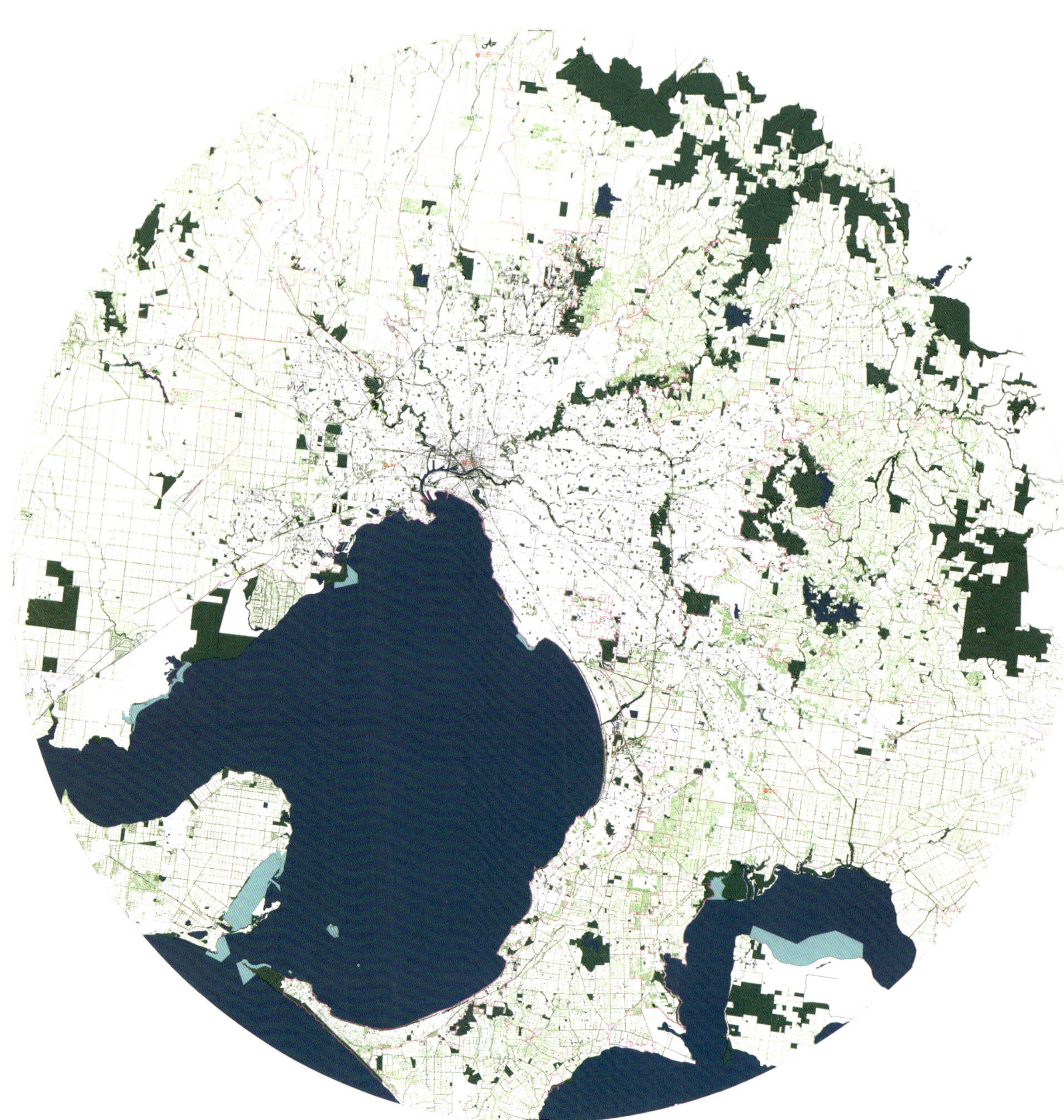

De-intensifying Consumption

The spatial consequences of our diet become clear when drawn as formal propositions for a whole city. This urban food proposition is simply not compatible with meat-intensive diets. Diet is familiar as a personal and public health issue; more recently its environmental impact has been scrutinised, particularly for the carbon footprint of meat production. Turning food production into an urban design and infrastructure problem makes this issue tangible, considered alongside housing, servicing, and other everyday problems of city making. Eating patterns translate directly to urban space, so the examination of diet for a productive self-sufficient city becomes crucial. The Australian diet is greater than the global average in terms of calories consumed. [13] Australia also has one of the highest rates of obesity in the developed world. [14] This contributes significantly to public health outcomes, but also to agricultural land use. The physical production footprint is overwhelmingly skewed to the production of meats, especially beef and lamb.[15] The EAT-Lancet reference diet (also known as the healthy reference diet) advocates far lower red meat consumption, with plant-based foods dominating the diet. This is typical nutritional health advice, and so has nutritional improvement effects, but also far lower land use and environmental impact. EAT-Lancet also refers to this diet as the planetary health diet as detailed in the EAT-Lancet Commission Brief for Cities report, which advocates urban agriculture. [16] By adopting the healthy reference diet, the amount of land required to feed Melbourne is dramatically reduced. Even using traditional agriculture methods, this requires less than half the current amount of land required to feed metropolitan Melbourne (approximately 5,483,000 hectares versus 11,676,000 hectares). [17] Using vertical high-density agricultural techniques and using the healthy reference diet as a production profile, the land requirement is further reduced. The foods advocated in the diet are also predominantly better suited to intensive production. A key project assumption is to adopt the healthy reference diet as a consumption model in Melbourne. Meat and dairy production (other than fish) has been excluded from the urban boundary of Melbourne as not feasible at scale. We might assume that meat remaining in the diet is sourced outside of this urban area and plant-based food production is generally the focus of our urban model. By adopting the healthy reference diet and excluding meat from urban production, we arrive at a figure of approximately 1,696,000 hectares of land required to feed the city. This is just under three times the calculated existing land available for production, suggesting that, with selective adoption of high-density vertical growing infrastructure, it is therefore possible to produce the majority of Melbourne's food requirements within its own footprint.

High-Density Growing Types

Testing models for growing food at high density in Melbourne's urban fabric. Vertical agricultural facilities were designed into various metropolitan conditions to form part of the total productive capacity and to form a viable part of the urban scene.

The project examines the design possibilities of a city driven by productive urban agricultural facilities. Calculations of population food demand and of available urban land set up the problem, which the designs speculate on. This project extends and builds on the Supertight project, which advocates for the qualities of hyper-dense cities. [18] Instead of infilling cities with more inhabitants, this project infills them with the production space needed to feed those inhabitants. The key outcomes of this study are investigations into new architectural types and their emergence within productive city environments. This is a speculative economy in which new architectural models might emerge. Using design as the key research tool, we have built on existing prototypes and agricultural modelling to project images of an urban architecture built around mass production of food at high density.

The architectural exploration of vertical farm objects is not new. Modern utopian city visions included agricultural production within the city limits. Ebenezer Howard's 1898 Garden City plan included space for (highly dispersed) large farms within its outer circle. [5.9]. Global urban population explosions, and developments in agricultural technology, including plant genetic modification, industrial lighting, and farm automation have fuelled increased interest in the architecture of vertical farms. Demonstration projects have been proposed around the world—from very small scales, such as The Greenhouse project in Federation Square in Melbourne, as shown in

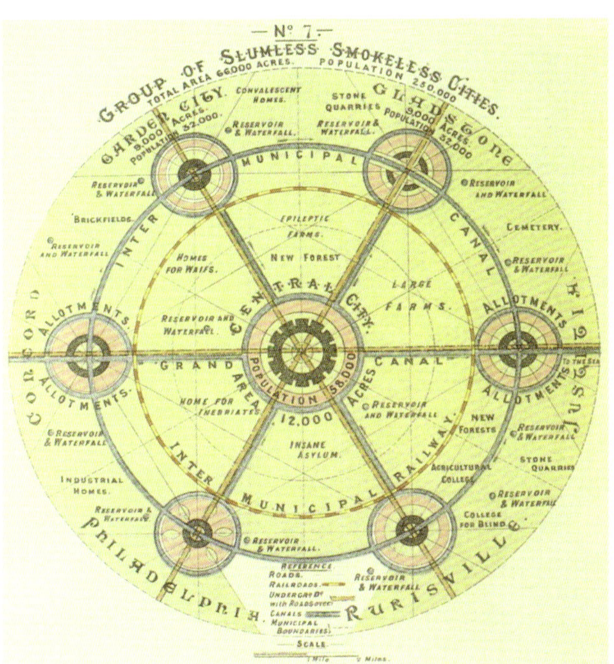

5.9 Garden City.

Ebeneezer Howard's Garden City proposal, including space within the middle ring for large farms.

5.10 Greenhouse at Federation Square.

Pop-up installation at Federation Square in Melbourne operating from 2008–2009, including food production and a restaurant.

5.10, to large agricultural production facilities, such as Shanghai's Sunqiao Urban Agriculture District, as shown in 5.11. Many present planting and greenery as dressing to the architecture. Planting as an architectural device has become a trope of 21st century design. A wave of speculative projects has projected an image of sustainability through planting, sometimes naïvely or even cynically. There are other social and psychological benefits of vegetation within cities and buildings, but there is less evidence of urban buildings where the economically viable mass food production has been designed along with a natural or ornamental appearance.

Real high-density agriculture is less glamorous—it is a food factory. Greenhouses might be viewed as the most common food factory example, although recently they have been augmented by industrial-scale hydroponic and aeroponic cultivation enclosed indoors under lights. Food factories have highly specific functional and spatial requirements: vast amounts of floor area with repeated racks for growing as efficiently as possible. Storage space, water supply, plant equipment, processing, packing, and shipping are significant portions of that area. Industrial meat, dairy, and egg production (more common today than high-density indoor plant production), requires space to house animals, for dairy milking, water and fodder storage, and waste removal systems. Many facilities have onsite slaughtering and packing areas. High-density agricultural production has specific environmental management systems. Controlled atmospheres for plants are critical for optimal growing. Animal facilities require sophisticated cooling and ventilation, along with containment of noise and odour.

Access and servicing are key considerations for high-density urban agriculture. Growing facilities consume considerable amounts of chemicals, produce voluminous plant quantities requiring frequent vehicle movements. Detailed specifications of these industrial facilities are complex and specialised. Technical requirements dominate design considerations, often dictated by engineers and specialists. The role of architecture in designing these (often) mute, optimised structures confronts this project. This urban scenario requires a large number of facilities that are varied in contents and distributed throughout the urban area. Typologically, they are an industrial shed, deployed in highly varied urban sites, at condensed scale and potentially adapted to be vertical.

Adapting existing redundant building types is another opportunity. The FarmHD project, as shown in 5.14, experimented in the context of Hong Kong China, identifying redundant multi-storey carparks that are generally difficult to adapt to habitation. Converting carparking structures to high-density plant growing complexes offers enormous agricultural volume and production capacity for reshaping Hong Kong China's food security profile. [19]

5.11 Sunqiao Urban Agriculture District.

Concept Design proposal for a new urban agriculture research and production facility in Shanghai.

5.12 Urban Agriculture.

High density greenhouses in the Netherlands have created a new form of non-human urbanism that has shaped the landscape.

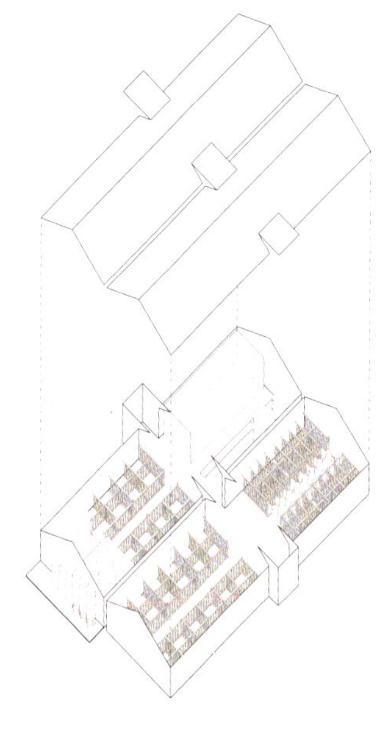

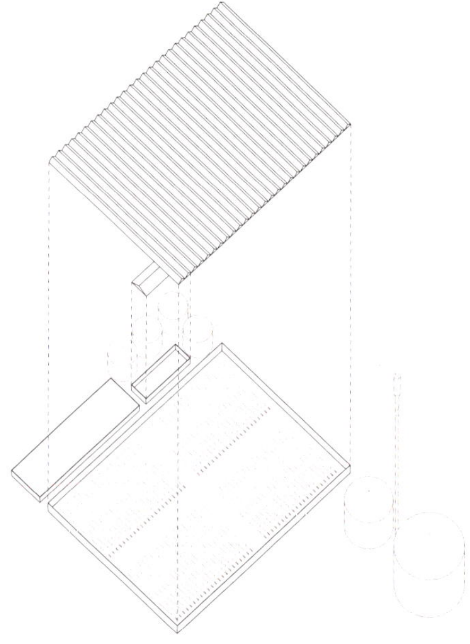

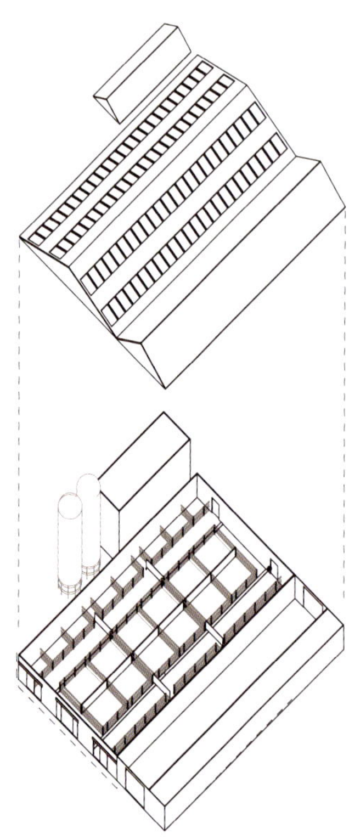

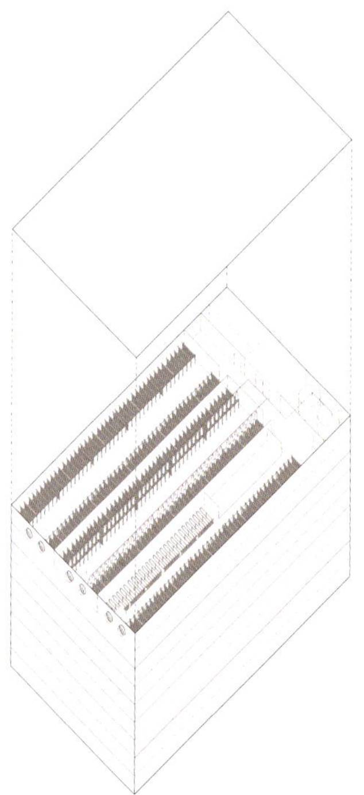

5.13 Intensive Agricultural Types.

A survey of the highest intensity form of production existing for each food type was undertaken. This catalogues a high intensity production type for various foods.

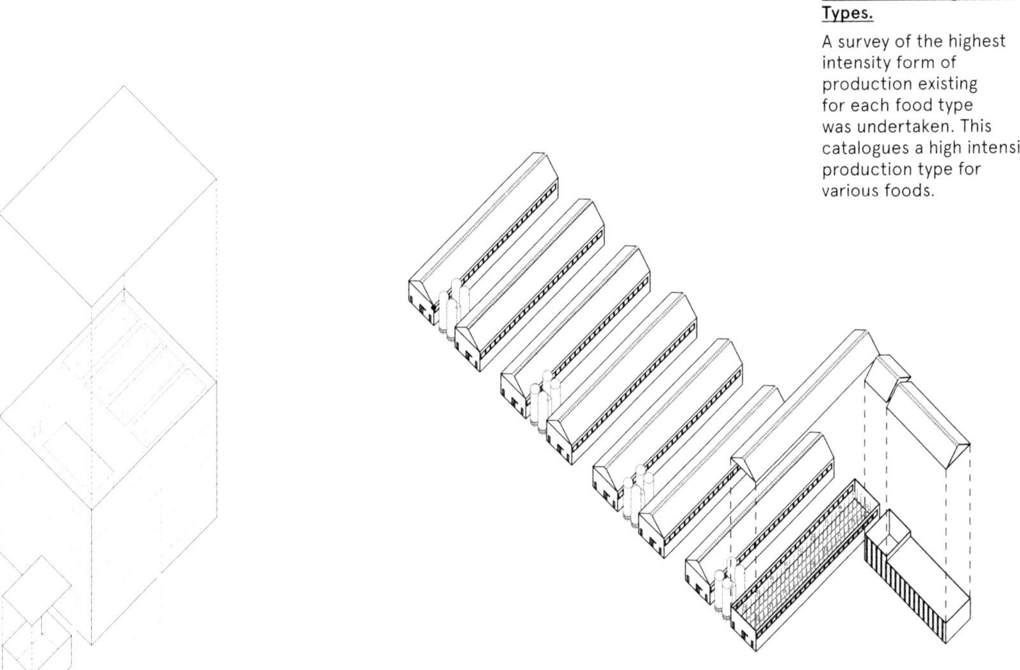

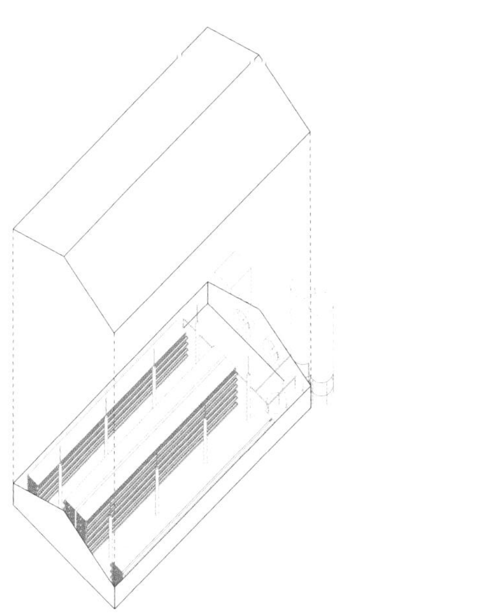

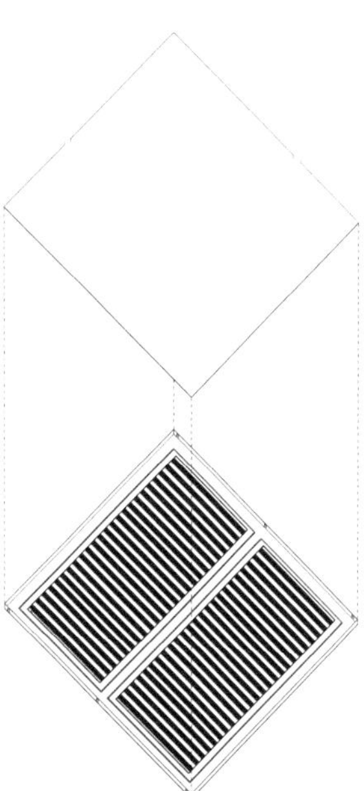

Inner city industrial heritage might also be a starting point for imagining a future food factory. Many cities are full of manufacturing remnants—artefacts of urban production before it moved to the metropolitan periphery and beyond. Ageing warehouses and factory buildings are valued for conversion, being finely composed and boldly scaled. These buildings precede modern mass transit systems and locate workforces close to workplaces. The limitations of inner urban production were offset by advantages in abundant labour—a compact that had the further effect of curtailing real estate speculation and land values.[20] Within such industrial heritage artefacts, the design problem of blank urban objects was well understood. The architecture of high-density factory farming similarly re-evaluates the orthodoxies of urban planning and design. Vertical farming functions frequently do not require daylight, which is impractical in deep-stacked floors. Blank façades are often inevitable.

Unanimated blank or undifferentiated façades set up interesting design possibilities or present other opportunities. Façades could be veneered with complementary programs such as housing with shallow floor plans forming skins with excellent daylight and ventilation, and animated built street edges. Vertical daylit growing space is another example. While not practical for the purposes of mass food production, a veneer of green space provides a form of perimeter animation, signalling, simultaneously, the use of the building in the city.

Other vertical farming types do not need fully enclosed envelopes. Greenhouses generally require temperature control; animal facilities require ventilation and acoustic control. However, areas of a vertical facility not used for controlled growing could be outside the envelope. Storage and processing sets up potential models where the envelope has no clear built edge. Free-range egg farms are an example. In some cases projects may be entirely without enclosed volume—a tight aggregate of infrastructural elements. Aquaculture farms are another example of this conception of the vertical farm taking on a field-like quality, a layered matrix of translucent, porous elements.

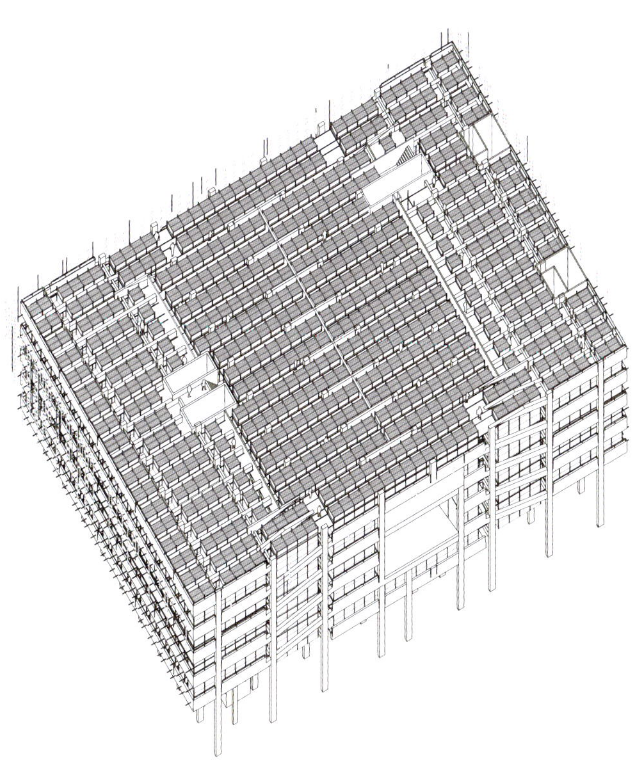

5.14 Farm HD.

An axonometric view of the Yau Mei Tai Municipal building in Hong Kong China converted into high-density growing space. Floor slabs have been removed allowing the volume of the structure to be filled with growing beds producing leafy greens.

5.15 Alphington Paper Mill.

An exterior photograph of The Alphington Paper Mill in suburban Melbourne (now demolished).

5.16 Free Range Chicken Farm.

A free range chicken farm, which is lined with netting to secure the birds, while allowing external sound and smells to permeate out to the surroundings.

Gresham St

Design Speculations

5.17 Inner City Agricultural Site.
Proposal for an ultra high-density growing facility located in the Central Business District of Melbourne.

The first design test of this urban agricultural proposition began with metropolitan- scale zoning maps to quantify available land. Land use mapping across the whole urban growth boundary identified potential sites and set out distribution of food growth areas. From this mapping, we identified four test precincts: 400 metre diameters where we tested architectural types in specific urban environments. The four precincts identified diverse work conditions. The first precinct is a high-rise context in the Melbourne central business district and existing multi-storey car parks for conversion. The second precinct is Brooklyn, a suburb ten kilometres west of the central business district of Melbourne, forming part of a low-rise territory of light industrial factory warehouses covering inner western suburbs. Wallan, the third precinct, sits at the northern extremity of the urban growth boundary. Still identifiable as a rural town on the highway to Victorian agricultural hinterlands, it now exists within the metropolitan land definition. The fourth precinct is Devon Meadows, which sits among peri-urban market gardens and orchards to the south-east.

In each instance, designs identified urban typological characteristics of the precinct and amplified these characteristics to house high-density agricultural production. In the central business district, the high-rise office tower form was replicated to hold farming rather than office space. The tower, dense with planting racks, was skinned with curtain walls and ornamental façade planting. It demonstrates the capacity of this ubiquitous model to be reappropriated for food production. In Brooklyn, the predominant existing model is large low-rise sheds, which we upgraded to three-storey height and laid out in a mat enclosure punctuated by courtyards admitting perimeter natural light and creating protected urban outdoor spaces. In Wallan, the simple strategy was to augment the dispersed collection of buildings. All that existed was retained and tall greenhouses were composed around them, re-invigorating the townscape, marking an edge to the metropolitan boundary and housing super-dense agriculture. The current agricultural focus at Devon Meadows is realised at greater intensity. High-yield greenhouse agriculture sat between, sometimes replacing fields of traditional orchard and pasture. In each case the urban model is not invented, but adapted and amplified.

In a second cycle of experiments, we focused on North Melbourne, a 19th century inner industrial suburb now gentrifying. We focused on buildings customised to particular infill sites within a context of positioning intensive production across North Melbourne. Three specialised produce models were tested: aquaculture, poultry and eggs, and green plants.

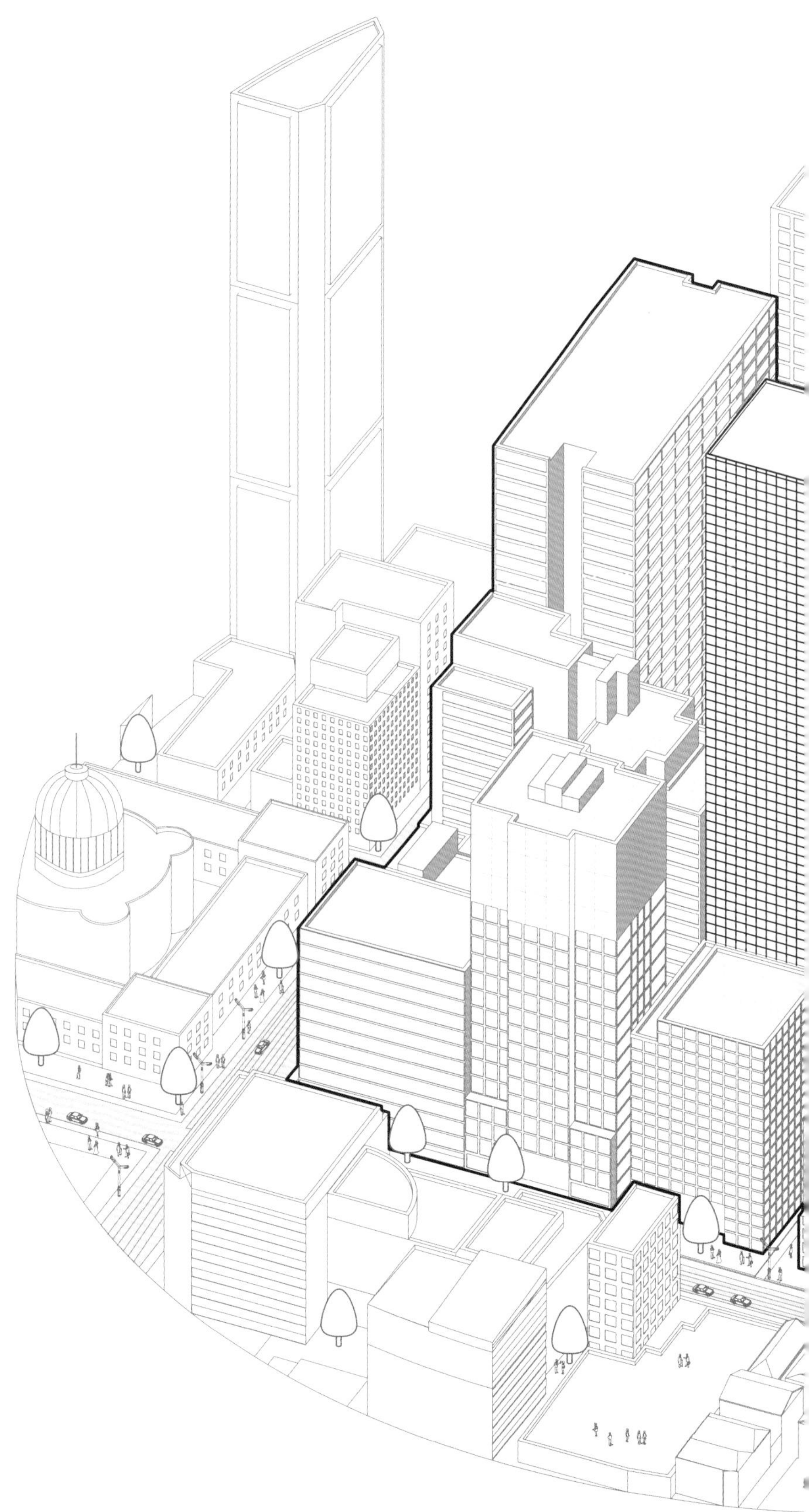

5.18 CBD Facility.

This proposal is for Melbourne's Central Business District. The project replaces an existing pair of multi-storey carparks. The floor area ratio matches that of adjacent office and residential towers.

5.19 At street level.

View of the Central Melbourne Agricultural Facility. The façade is veneered with planting, creating a green envelope to the facility which is populated with densely packed growing beds under artificial lights.

5.20 Elevation View.

The full height of the Central Melbourne Agricultural Facility as a part of a broader field of towers in the city.

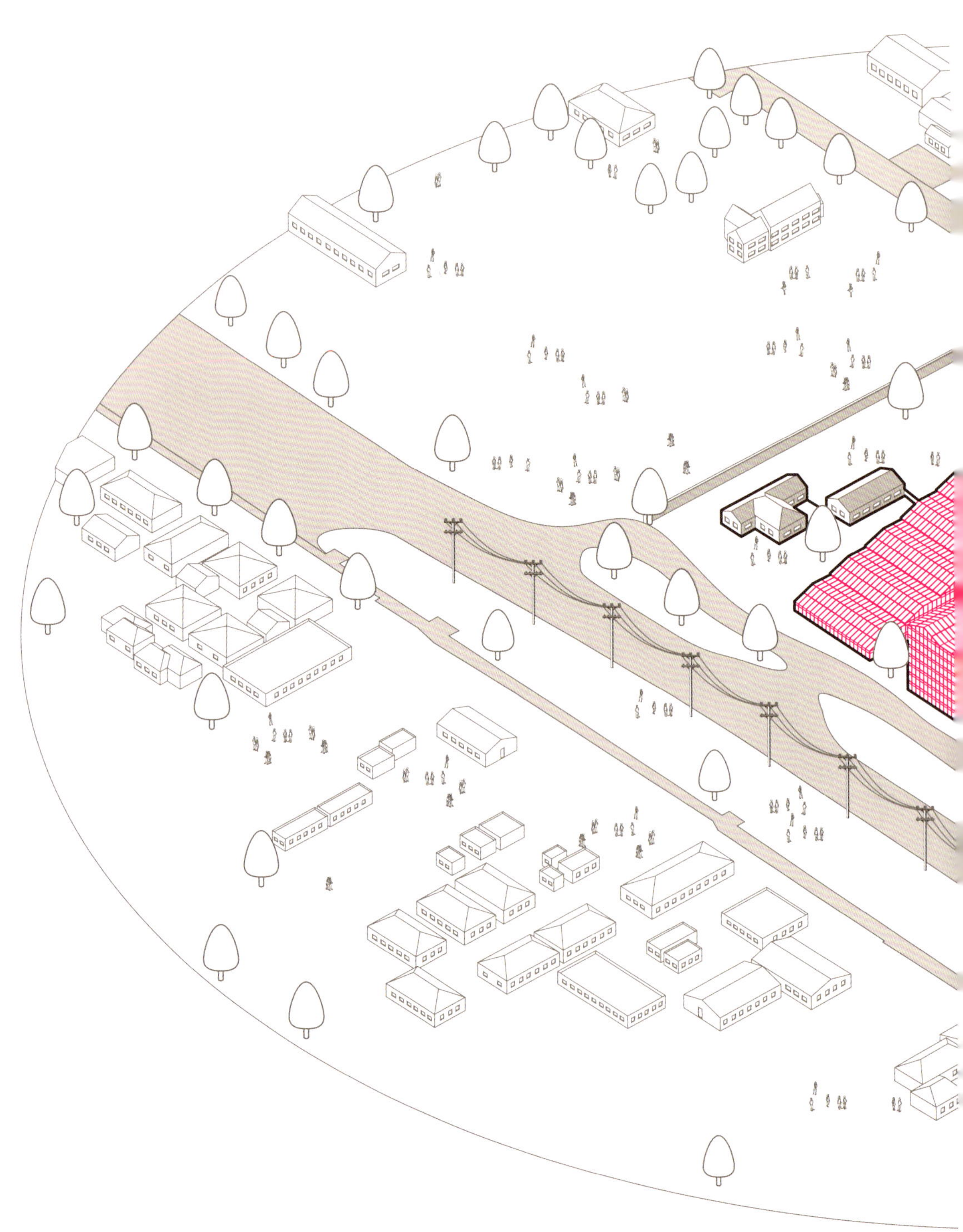

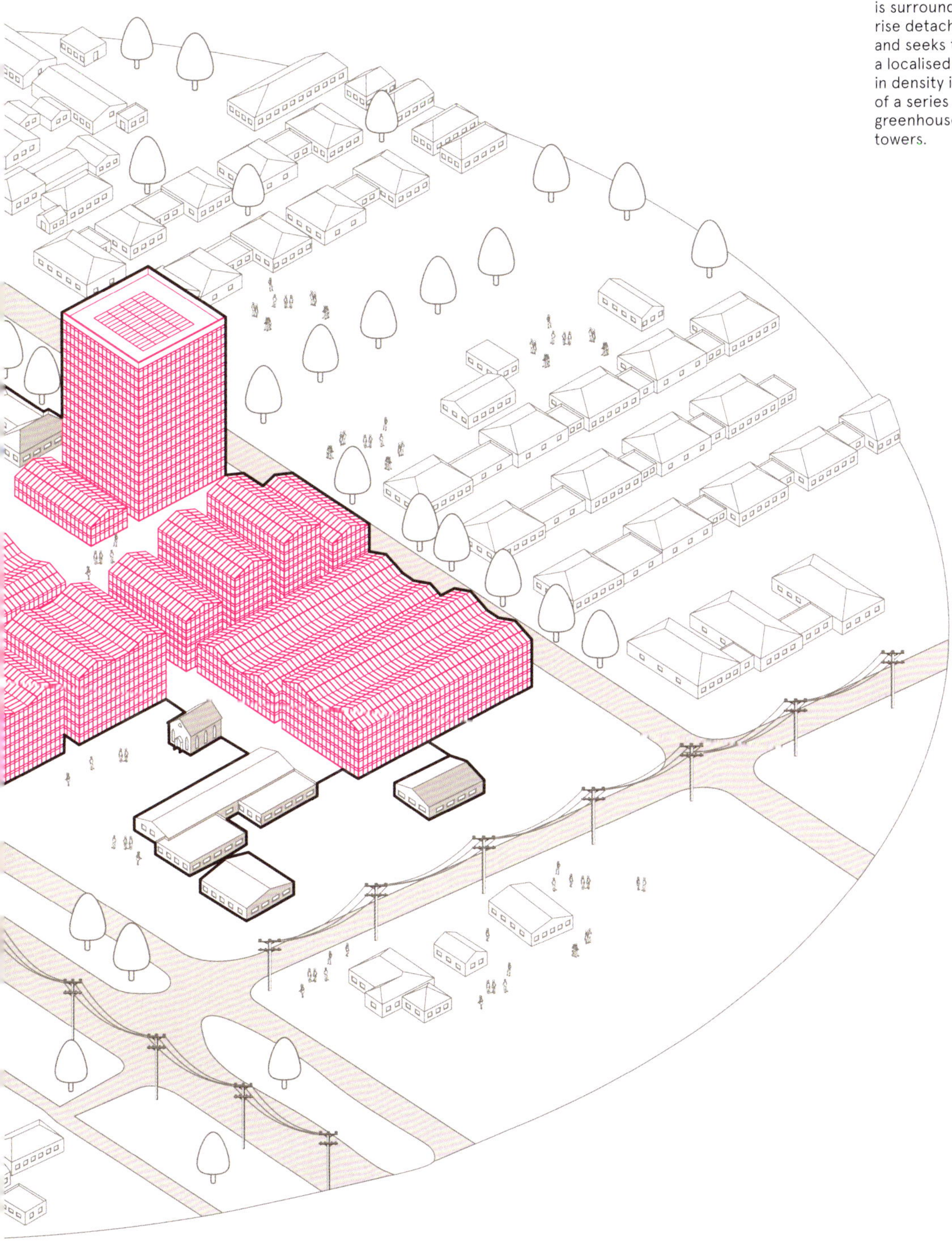

5.21 Wallan Facility.

This proposal is for the outer edge of Melbourne's urban growth boundary to the north. The facility sits in the suburb of Wallan, a former agricultural town that has been absorbed into the metropolitan boundary. The proposal is surrounded by low rise detached houses and seeks to provide a localised increase in density in the form of a series of vertical greenhouses and growing towers.

5.22 Civic Infrastructure.

The Wallan project sits near a small 19th century church. The forecourt of the church is currently used on weekends as an informal marketplace. The proposal leverages this existing condition to create a permanent 'farmers market' selling goods from the greenhouse and a series of community garden beds using traditional growing techniques.

5.23 Scale Shift.

The project is a notable scale shift from the surrounding suburb. It draws on the vernacular language of the large footprint shed, common to the outer suburbs. The impact of this is softened by the use of transparent or translucent envelope materials. A large portion of the food grown at this facility would be under daylight.

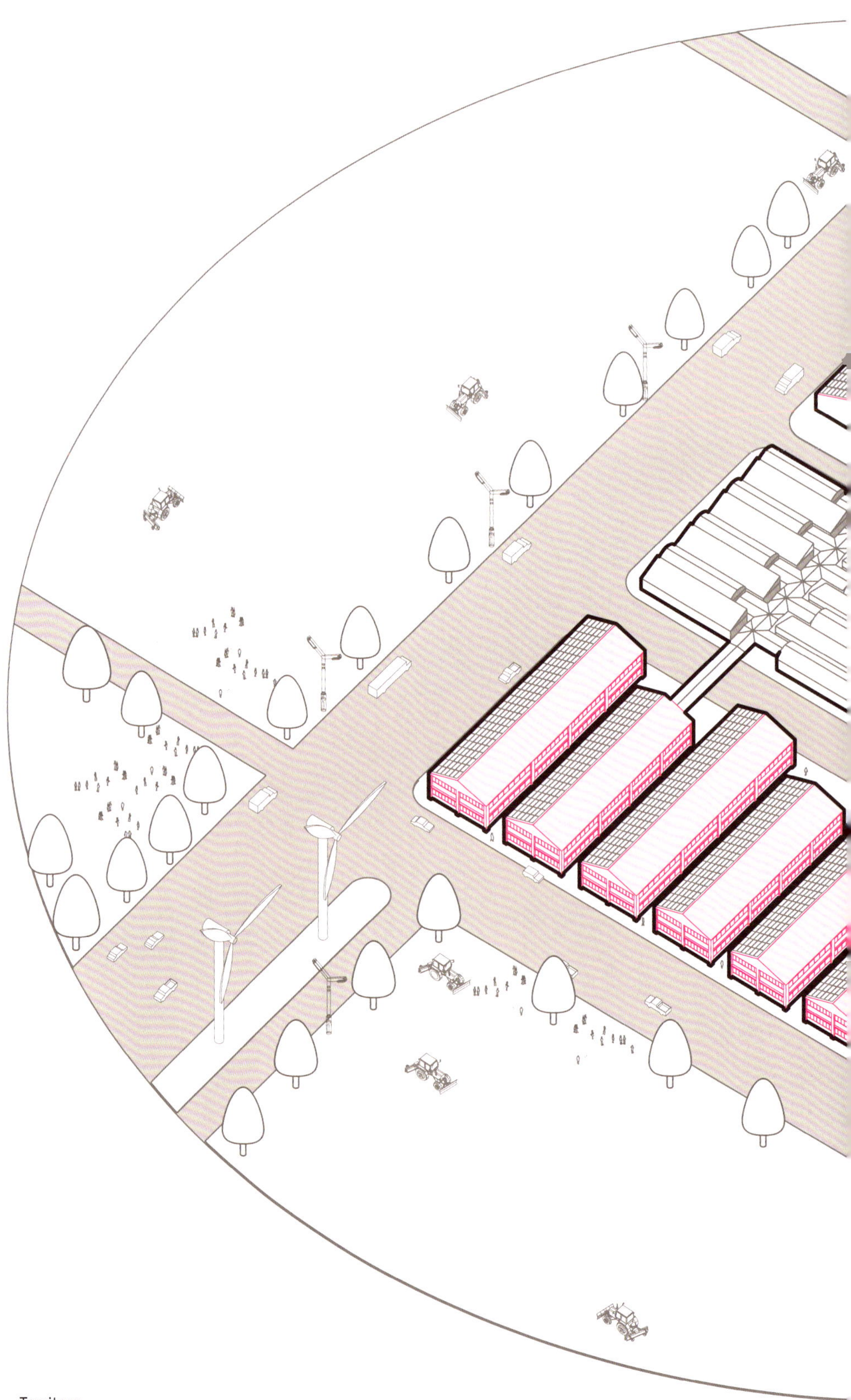

5.24 Devon Meadows Facility.

This proposal sits at the eastern periphery of Melbourne, on land that is currently used for agriculture—vegetables and pasture. The expanding development of housing in this area continually threatens productive agricultural land.

5.25 Incremental Intensification.

The ambition of the Devon Meadows project is to demonstrate incremental intensification of agricultural production on land already used for growing food.

5.26 Low-Rise High-Rise.

The design is comprised of a series of low rise 1–2 storey traditional greenhouses, allowing the intensification of fruit and vegetable production. These buildings are the scale of existing sheds on the site. The overall density and yield of the site is increased through the inclusion of vertical growing towers, which are modelled on the grain silo type commonly found in rural Australian towns. The inclusion of a single point of high-density production offsets the remainder of the site and allows for a modest scale overall.

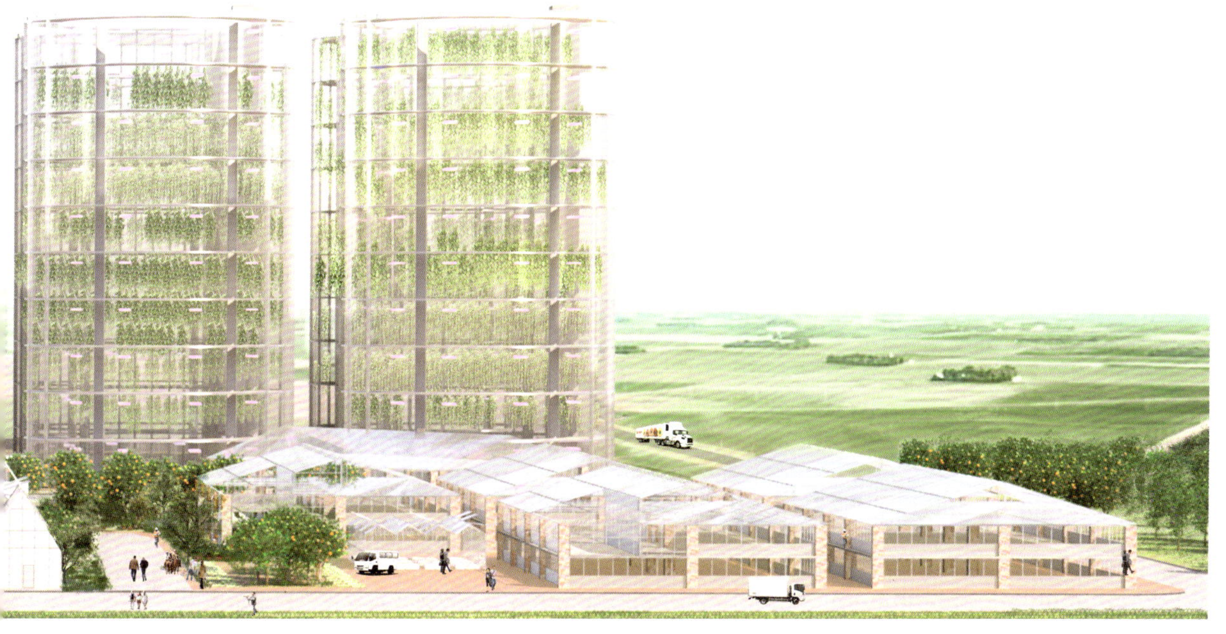

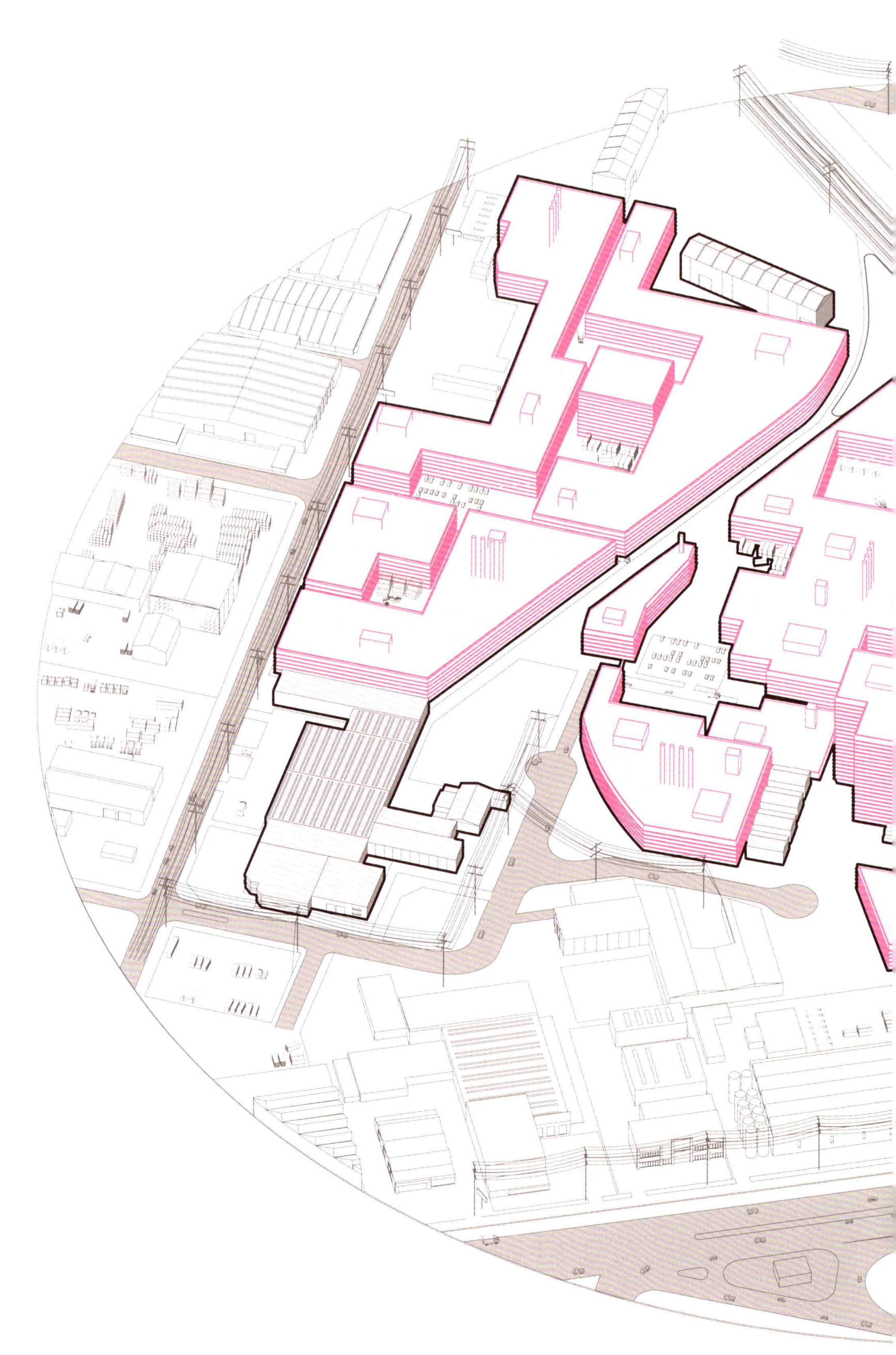

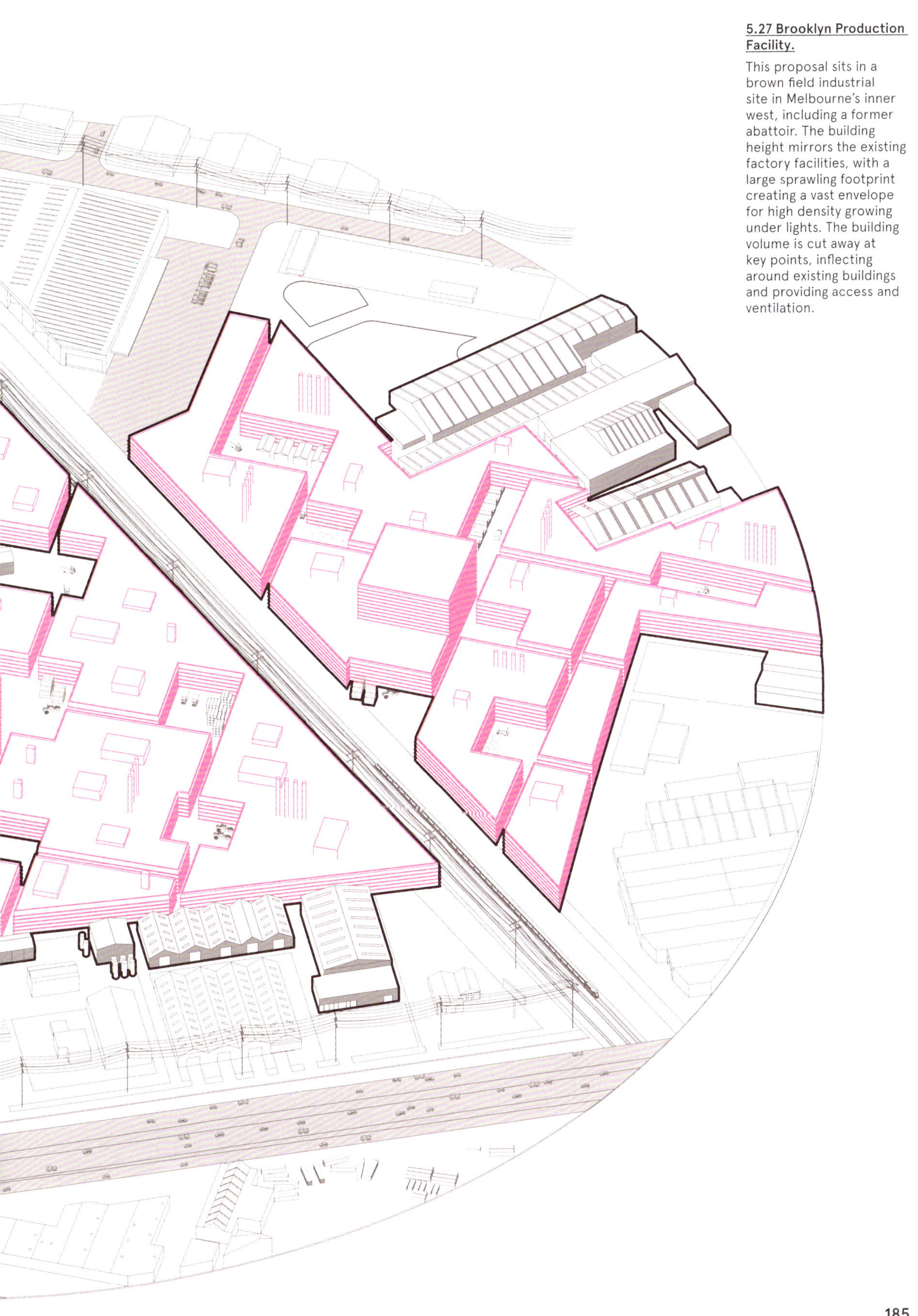

5.27 Brooklyn Production Facility.

This proposal sits in a brown field industrial site in Melbourne's inner west, including a former abattoir. The building height mirrors the existing factory facilities, with a large sprawling footprint creating a vast envelope for high density growing under lights. The building volume is cut away at key points, inflecting around existing buildings and providing access and ventilation.

5.28 Almost Business as Usual.

The Brooklyn proposal explores the most probable architectural future for urban food production—one which is already appearing in cities around the world. It is a vast, non-descript industrial facility hidden behind closed gates in which extensive quantities of food are produced.

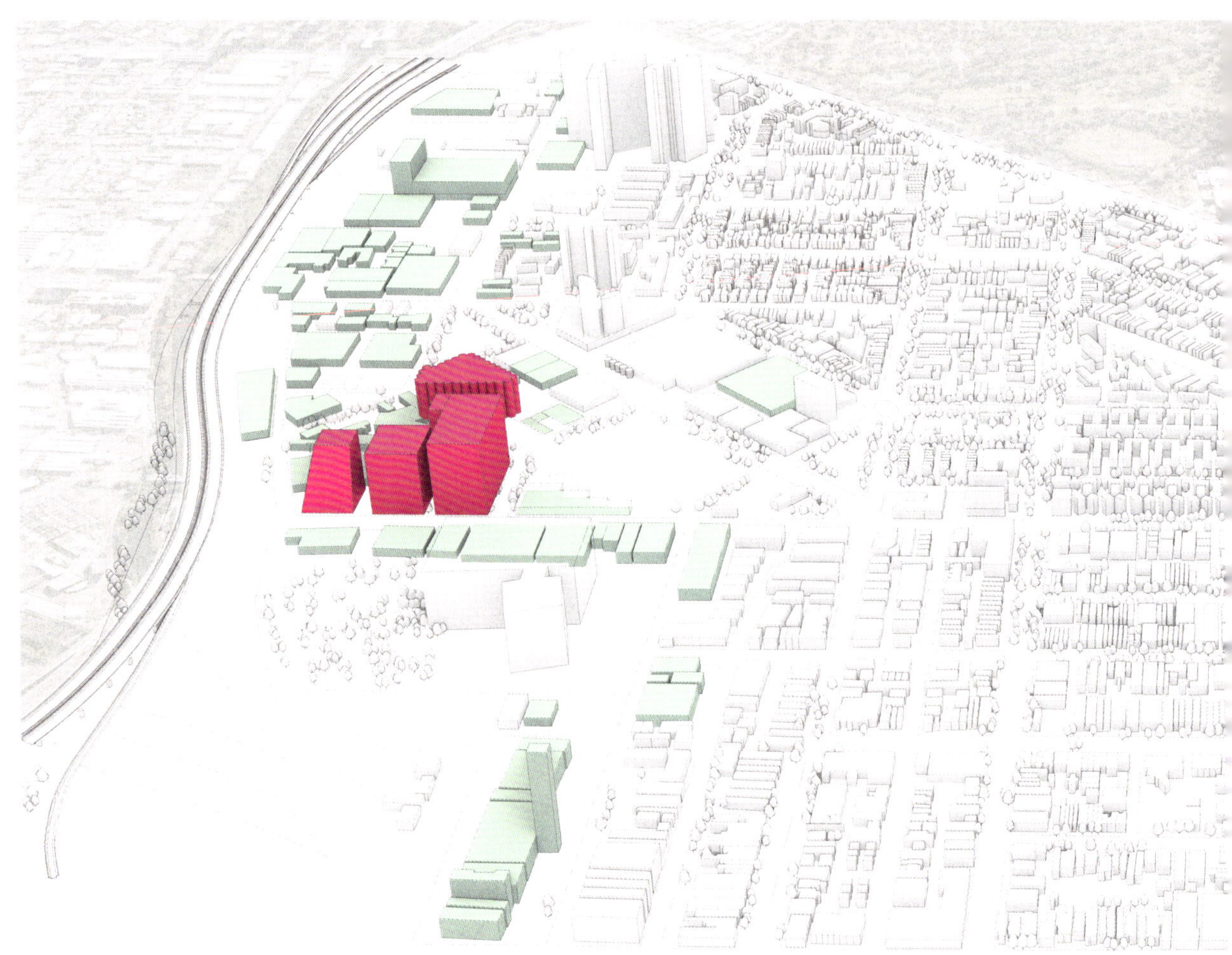

5.29 Aerial View of North Melbourne.

This view captures the extents of the suburb of North Melbourne. Potential sites for high-intensity agriculture are identified in green. The sites tested through design projects in the following pages are shown in pink.

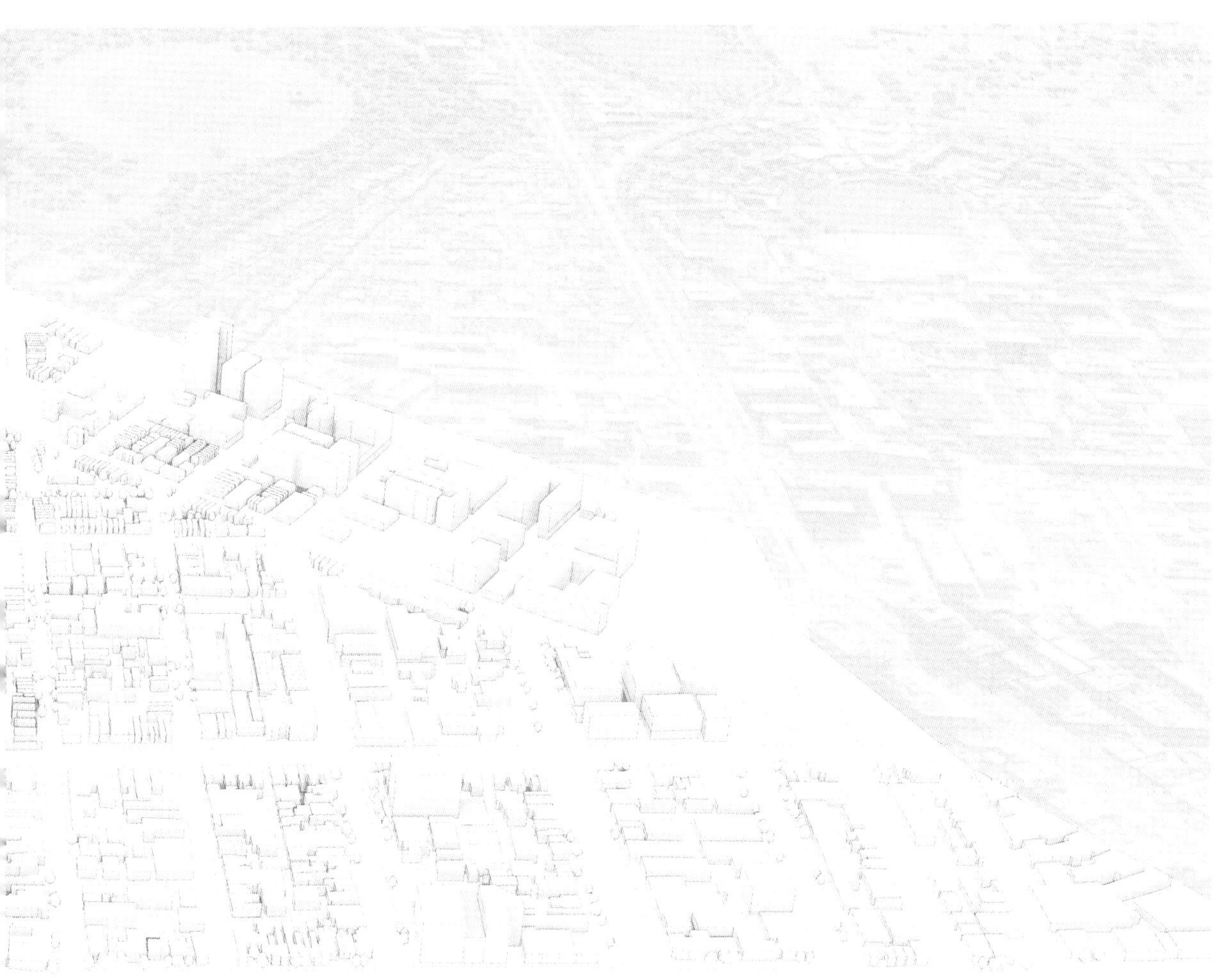

Finally, a mixed production model was developed finding its design expression in variegated use. Unlike the mute enclosures of intensive production, this type aims to activate the future 10–20 storey urban landscape. The precinct used is North Melbourne, a former industrial district and location for a new underground metro station. The area is projected to mix high-density residential, commercial, and healthcare developments over the next decades.

The proposal combines tactics from earlier typological experiments into an agricultural complex producing vegetables, fruits, and grains indoors under controlled conditions, with rooftop orchards providing soil-based planting for nut trees. The building's basement hosts aquaculture producing fish varieties along with water storage and plant. Each food type accommodates different growing requirements in separate volumes. The design serves as a direct outlet to the public, providing walk-up access to growing areas for purchase where produce is grown. A large public mezzanine connects directly to street frontage facilities and provides further community garden space and small market stalls.

This design's ambition is to test the limits of the vertical growing facility as an urban type. The majority of the interior building volume is given to growing space—planting racks, fish tanks, and equipment, storage, and plant. The building has little requirement for natural light or external views and could be, like the industrial examples previously described, mute externally. In approaching this design we sought to experiment with this muteness, simultaneously amplifying and celebrating it, while challenging it. The starting point was a series of production spaces built to the maximum envelope, these volumes were pushed up and set back to allow for public space proceeding from the street level, and for vertical circulation corridors that provide direct access to the production spaces of the building. Each production volume is treated as distinct, with its own address and access point, creating highly active exterior circulation.[21]

The design experiments with different forms of muteness, achieving layered forms of enclosure. The building's façade mixes different systems with varied visual and environment porosity. Perforated steel mesh envelopes the top third of the building, enclosing rice production space. This screen reads as solid and blank during daylight and allows internal light to glow from the planting lights at night.

Varied glazed façades wrap the lower production levels. A large plane of glazing spanning between the vegetable and fruit volumes is intended to read as a cut section revealing the volume's contents. This approach allows visual access to the interior, revealing little human occupation and a wall of industrial agricultural fittings. Through the side rear of the fruit and vegetable volumes, varied bays of polycarbonate glazing panels give differing aspects into the building—some clear and direct, others diffuse and shadowy.

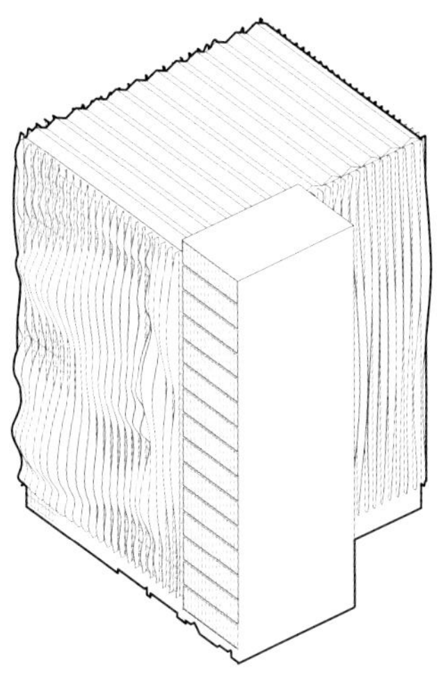

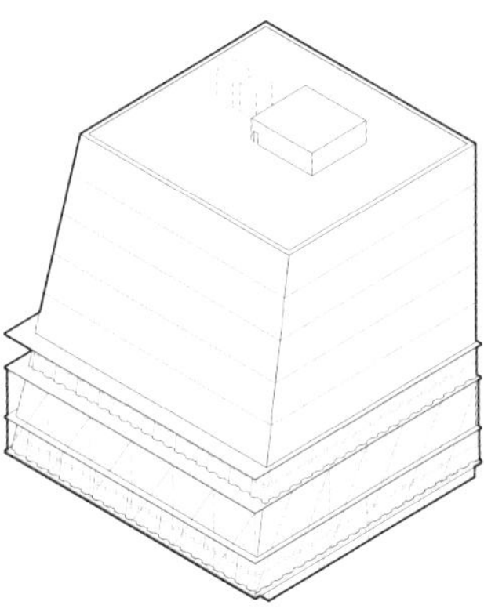

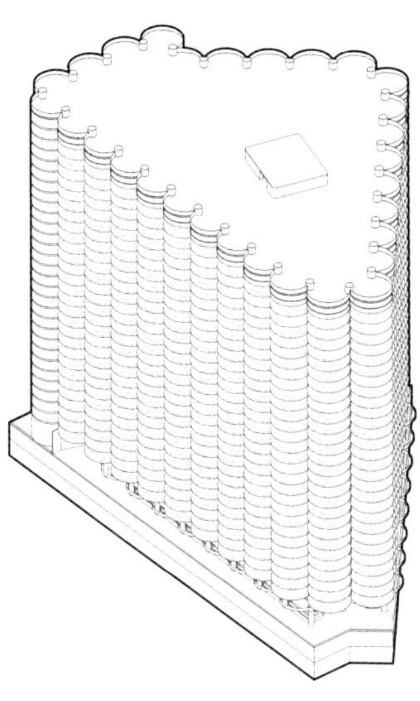

5.30 Experiments in Growing Types.

A series of design experiments into different vertical agriculture typologies. From top to bottom: a vertical greenhouse growing fruit and vegetables under lights with a louvred glass façade provides visual access to the food production; a high-density chicken meat and egg production facility includes a series of layered façades allowing ventilation while limiting visual access to the facility; a vertical aquaculture facility where the intense structural requirements of stacked tanks provides a language to the façade of the building.

5.31 Demonstration Project.

An exterior of the demontration project from Arden Street in North Melbourne. The project is a vertical stack of different agricultural production types, with direct public access and civic space.

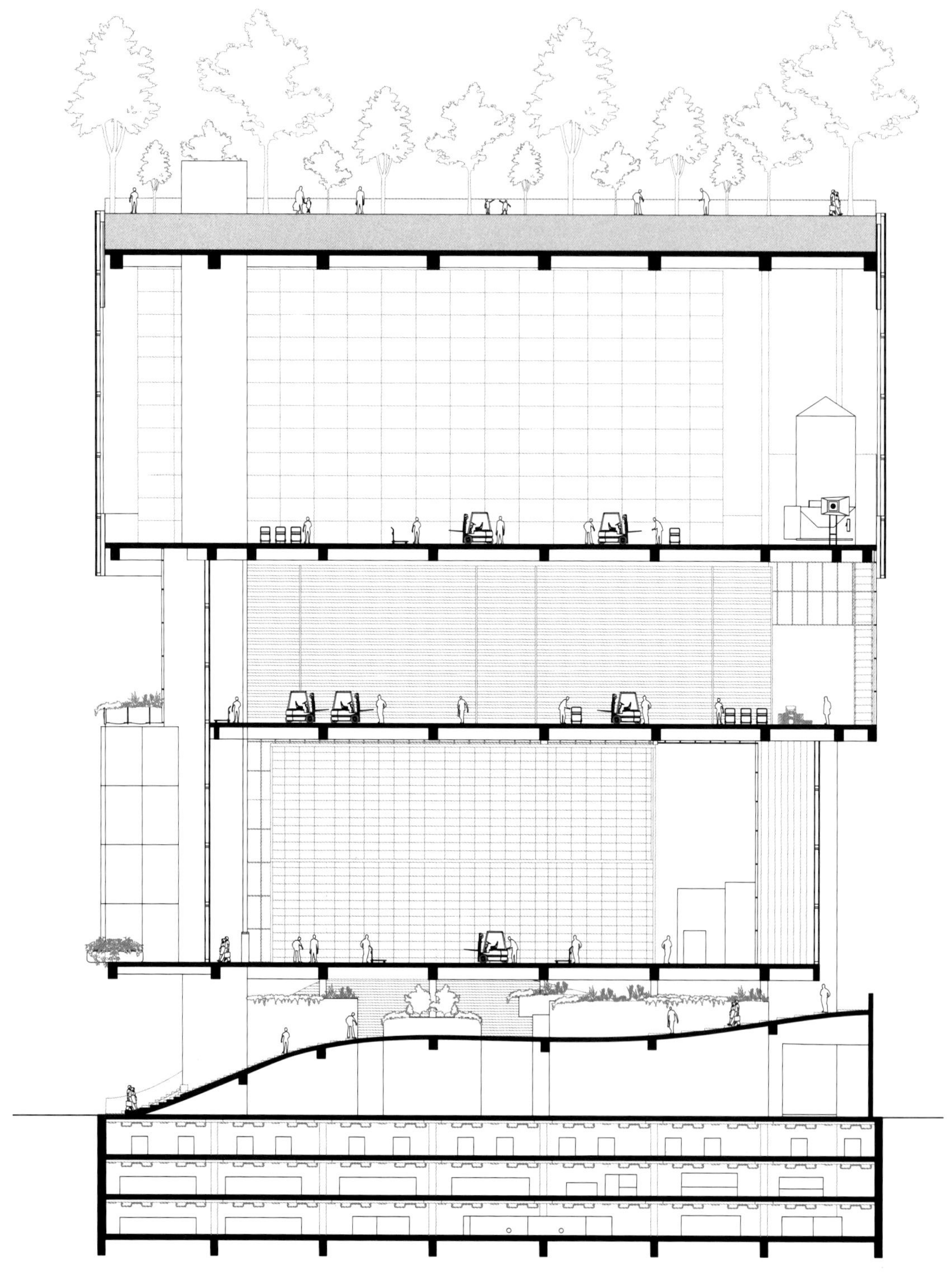

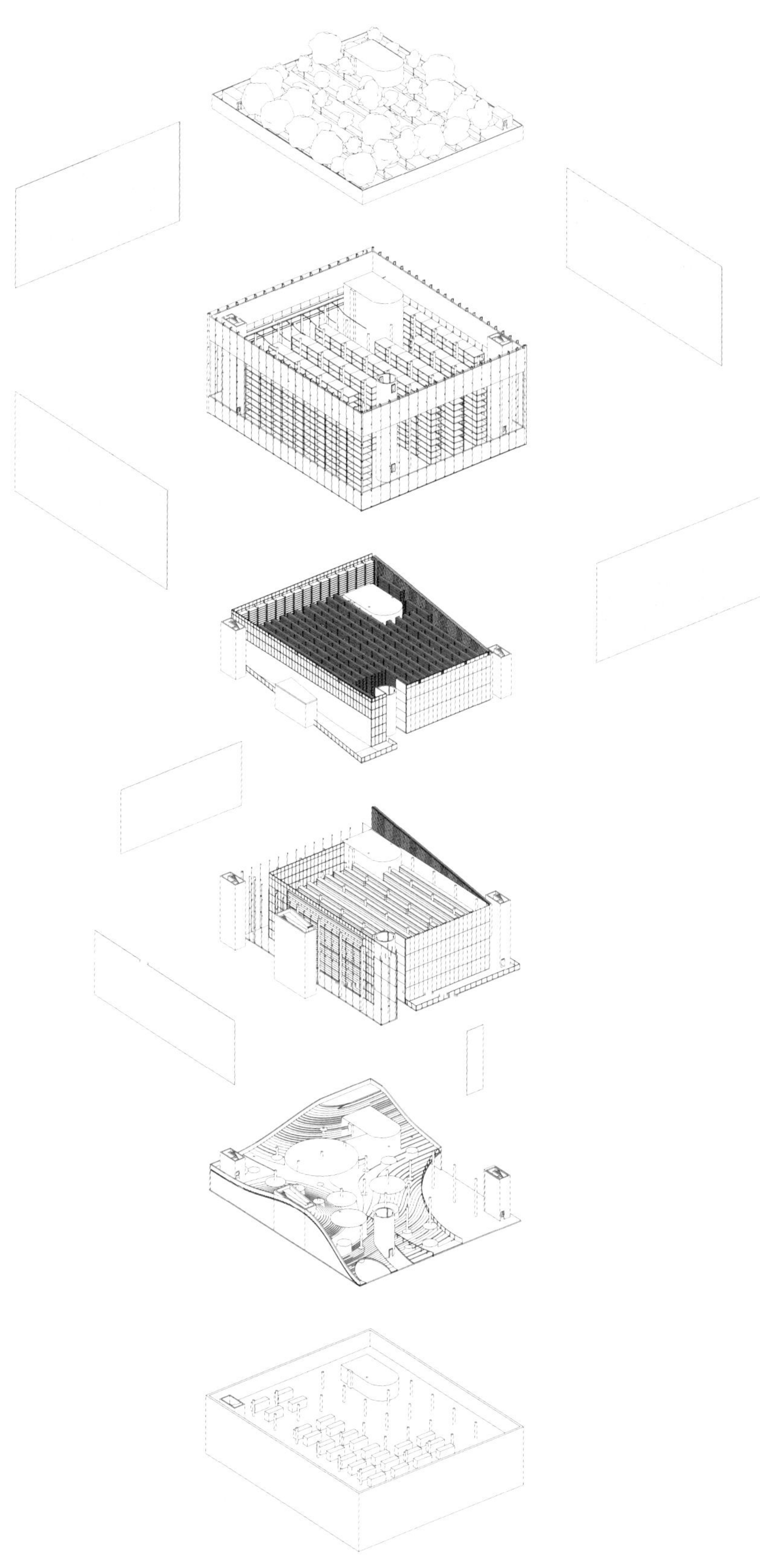

5.32 Building Section.

(left): Section through the proposal indicating the diverse range of production facilities, secondary plant and equipment, and social or civic spaces.

5.33 Exploded Isometric Drawing.

The proposal illustrating the organisation of the project's various functions.

5.34 At Street Level.

A view of the growing tower in North Melbourne from street level indicating a public plaza and mezzanine with direct access up to the growing levels of the building.

5.35 Growing Levels.

A view of the typical growing racks against the external façades for the North Melbourne project.

Public access to the fruit and vegetable production volumes comes through terraces accessed via stairs and ramps. A lightweight curtain separates interior and exterior spaces, which would be impossible if the type were intended for human habitation. The use of mesh and open curtain façades provides layered depth to the building envelope. Some storage and packing areas are left entirely open to the elements, with conditioned spaces limited to growing areas requiring environmental control. Melbourne's temperate climate allows growing spaces to potentially be open to the environment for much of the year, subject to bio-security requirements. This sets up the intriguing possibility of smell and sound leaking from the facility. While city dwellers are accustomed to the hum of equivalent urban infrastructures and traffic, a truly novel experience might be the smell of fresh food growing. The aroma of tomatoes growing could fill the neighbourhood, while petals falling from almond and walnut trees could drift down to the street in late winter.

While this project is entirely speculative, and issues of economic feasibility have only loosely been interrogated, the design experiment proves the potential for dense urban agriculture to not only fulfil food production needs, but to operate as civic infrastructure.

What does it mean when a significant proportion of city space is dedicated, for the first time, to farming? Melbourne is a low-density metropolis with a very large urban boundary, making this proposition viable. The modelling for this project assumed no loss of residential land or green space. The strategy takes up big areas of low-intensity land use and infills high-intensity farming. This infill includes area of former manufacturing and so inner and middle portions of the city consolidate without gaining population density. Suburban houses and gardens are unaffected, except that those households are more likely to buy food grown or made nearby. Melbourne's urban growth boundary contains significant areas which are rural or undeveloped, and these areas would see construction of greenhouses and rural sheds on a significant scale.

In some ways, this project is a return to a once prevalent urban condition. Warehouses and factories are retained for new manufacturing instead of being converted to housing; sites are developed for food manufacturing at a scale comparable to early 20th century production. Land nominally urban in the vague periphery is re-asserted as rural and its agricultural activity amplified.

The Urban Implications of a Self-Feeding City

The logistical implications of this productive re-distribution are significant. Trucking produce into cities and across cities creates an entire infrastructural industry around road transport. In this urban model far more food is sold (and even eaten) at the growing source and so more food is purchased at a walkable distance from home.

In many cities, there is anxiety around the health of food sources, whether by contamination of soils and water, chemical additives, or animal cruelty. The disconnect between food consumption and production and the visibility of food sources is an intensifying issue. One implication of agriculture in cities is simply that our food could be more visible. Would seeing our food growing change how it is made? This visibility connects with the urban design convention for street activation. A city filled with large agricultural industrial buildings can be activated with market outlets, and visible production, thus enlivening street edges.

This urban proposition says little about the capacity for food production at the domestic scale; the thousands of small productive gardens that exist and remain possible within the suburban housing stock. This project complements that, focusing on the commercial and industrial scale of food.

What could this urban production mean for the rural hinterland? The rural areas beyond Melbourne are under intense pressure. They are threatened by metropolitan sprawl and climate change, and they in turn threaten natural environments. Rural towns are pressured by depopulation and yet they represent a significant export industry. Three scenarios spring from urban agriculture. First, declining rural towns take on the same logic of intensifying their agricultural footprint as means to consolidating or reviving their own regional place. Second, large-scale land resources are freed to focus on export activity focused on bulk grain or pasture. That is, traditional agriculture complements the urban farm. Third, the reforestation and reversal of the environmental damage from agriculture can take place where low-intensity rural land is replaced by intensive growing.

5.36 Public Access.

A view from a publicly accessible balcony at the upper growing levels. Members of the public can purchase procuce directly from the growers.

5.37 High-Intensity Growing Space.

An interior view of the growing spaces as they transition into public retail outlets—a mediation between human and non-human space.

01
02

5.[illegible]8 Non-Human Landscapes.

High intensity agriculture under lights with artificial growing beds can be largely automated with existing technology. This creates a future landscape where human use and comfort are not the primary design criteria. What will these spaces look like, how might they be designed and what is their contribution to the city?

Reflections

We have run several iterations of designs in various urban situations. These iterations demonstrate the inflection of design models within the spectrum of metropolitan conditions, as well as the variety of possible expressions within the city.

We have calculated a total agricultural footprint based on demand, which equates to an average of three floors for each new or converted growing facility. This profile though would vary dramatically, just as metropolitan development currently varies in its cross section. The intention is to mirror the general metropolitan form and to intensify it. In a similar way, the project does not presume necessarily a new model of ownership for food production. It is conceivable that the current highly concentrated ownership of supermarkets in Australia could persist in an urban production model.

This project aims to redesign an urban system that makes food remote from a city and transports it in. It also aims to demonstrate, through design, the capacity of the city to absorb that production and to design compatible models. It does that within the general metropolitan form and profile of low-to-medium density housing and with extensive green reserves. Its focus on the urban design models means financial or economic models are open to many possibilities.

Finally, the self-feeding city project provokes consideration of the entire urban food demand. Like all major urban moves, it is incremental and possible partially. Rather than an all or nothing proposition, it is our contention that urban environments would benefit from any increased local food production. Even the tightest city has a massive footprint of hinterland servicing its food consumption. This project imagines and designs a tightly productive metropolis, with enough agricultural surface area to feed the city population and without losing housing or green space. The hinterland beyond is left for better use and the urban objects that result (food factories) are woven into the city's scale and texture.

Endnotes

1. See Crist, G. and J. Doyle. Supertight: Models for Living and Making Culture in Dense Urban Environments. Barcelona: Aktar, 2021.
2. Visontay, E. "Three reasons why Melbourne's population will overtake Sydney's within a decade", The Guardian, Thursday, Jan 5, 2023, https://www.theguardian.com/australia-news/2023/jan/05/three-reasons-why-melbournes-population-will-overtake-sydneys-within-a-decade.
3. Australian Bureau of Statistics. Regional population: statistics about the population for Australia's cities and regions. 2022, https://www.abs.gov.au/ausstats/abs@.nsf/mf/3218.0.
4. University of Melbourne Victorian Eco Innovation Lab. Melbourne Foodprint Report. 2016.
5. Statista. Land used to produce one kilogram of food product as of 2018, by type. 2018, https://www.statista.com/statistics/1179708/land-use-per-kilogram-of-food-product/.
6. See Department of Infrastructure. Draft Melbourne 2030: Planning for Sustainable Growth. Melbourne. 2002, https://www.planning.vic.gov.au/__data/assets/pdf_file/0017/100718/Urban-Growth-Boundary.pdf.
7. Victorian Department of Environment, Land, Water, and Planning. DataShare. 2017, https://datashare.maps.vic.gov.au/search?q=uuid%3D0ba63dff-edac-5a95-99af-1cd616a81f76.
8. This compares our calculation of available metropolitan land with the baseline requirement for current consumption.
9. Aerofarms (https://www.aerofarms.com) is one of numerous innovators in high-density production techniques.
10. For example, Lam, S., G. Pham, and H. Nguyen-Viet. Emerging health risks from agricultural intensification in Southeast Asia: a systematic review. International Journal of Occupational and Environmental Health, 2017, Jul; 23(3): 250–260.
11. Poore, J. and Nemecek, T. Additional calculations by Our World in Data. 2018, www.OurWorldInData.org/environmental-impacts-of-food.
12. We have assumed that varied crops are produced at comparable yields to known facilities.
13. Our World in Data. Daily Caloric Supply (OWID based on UN FAO & historical source). https://ourworldindata.org/grapher/daily-per-capita-caloric-supply?tab=table.
14. https://www.oecd.org/els/health-systems/Obesity-Update-2017.pdf
15. Poore, J. and T. Nemecek. Additional calculations by Our World in Data. 2018, www.OurWorldInData.org/environmental-impacts-of-food.
16. OECD. Obesity Update 2017. https://eatforum.org/lancet-commission/cities.
17. This is calculated using equivalent yield areas for the proportion of category intake in each diet profile.
18. Crist, G. and J. Doyle. Supertight: Models for Living and Making Culture in Dense Urban Environments. Barcelona: Aktar, 2021.
19. Crist, G and J. Doyle. FarmHD symposium CUHK, Hong Kong, China, 2016.
20. Melbourne is typical of large cities where dispersal of both manufacturing and housing accelerated from the mid 20th century. Most inner urban industrial areas are gentrifying to residential.
21. This approach borrows from the contradictions of the Alphington's paper mill's public interface. A blank façade that is animated through a very active public exchange point between the largely mechanised productive internal operations of the facility and the urban realm.

Dialogue with Areti Markopoulou: Growing Tight Food

This chapter is a transcript of a discussion held via video conference on 28 October 2022 between Areti Markopoulou from the Institute for Advanced Architecture of Catalonia and the members of the Productive Cities research team comprising Dr Silvia Micheli, Associate Professor Antony Moulis and Dr Peyman Akhgar of The University of Queensland's School of Architecture; Dr John Doyle and Associate Professor Graham Crist of RMIT University's School of Architecture and Urban Design; and Dongwoo Yim and Dr Rafael Luna, co-founders of the architecture firm PRAUD.

The discussion took place during the early stages of this publication and centred around the Growing Tight Food project, specifically focusing on the value of speculative projects to address the broader social, economic and regulatory implications of high-density urban agriculture. Discussions focused on the value of the project as a speculative scenario, and sought to unpack the broader social, economic, regulatory, and other implications of the mass adoption of high-density urban agriculture.

Graham Crist:
The work we are presenting in this publication spun off from the Supertight project, which was examining very high-density and micro elements within cities. In the course of this project, we became aware that every city, including high-density cities, has a hinterland that forms the shadow of a city's footprint. Working from this we became interested in understanding how cities might begin to incorporate productive functions within high-density urban environments. Our project specifically examines how the food production requirements of a city such as Melbourne can be completely accommodated within its metropolitan boundary. We're asking what is possible, knowing that it's an improbable provocation. If 100% of a city's food needs were met within the boundary, particular conditions are required for that to happen. Even if 50% or 20% occurred within the boundary, it would be quite a significant impact on the city.

John Doyle:
In an earlier project we looked at the multi-storey carpark as one type which will be redundant in the next 10 or 20 years. It's one example of how adaptive re-use might be implemented at the architectural scale for urban agriculture. Multi-storey carparks and urban agriculture are both mute industrial programs. We've been interested in reframing urban agriculture from a typological perspective as something which might have a civic role or perform as civic infrastructure in the city. It might do something or be designed in a way that it interfaces with the city in a desirable fashion.

Areti Markopoulou:
It is very interesting to see that the inner middle portions of Melbourne are consolidating without increasing in population. In your project, suburban housing is not affected. Urban growth continues to expand into rural areas, but food is produced locally. However, I observe that the proposition seems

apologetic, and takes as granted the hypothesis that not much changes should happen, as if the less change proposed is the most appropriate solution.

I understand that this project is a speculation based on rigorous analysis, but if we depart from the urgent need on producing fundamental changes in how we inhabit, plan, consume or operate as citizens, it is imperative to be much more radical in how we implement these changes that will boost new models in cities.

I appreciate the smoothness and I appreciate that this might be a good way to introduce such a project to policy makers, decision makers or different authorities. But I do feel that we need to have a more radical perspective on how we re-think our buildings, not only adapting or retrofitting the existing ones.

We need to change our habits and the perspective of the city, not only our diets. It is extremely interesting that in your proposal, the buildings contribute to civic infrastructure. What does it mean to create a civic infrastructure of the 21st century and beyond? Which citizens are we addressing with these ideas? Over the last two hundred years, the way infrastructure has been built has been only focusing on human needs and the commodities they need to fulfill certain standards of lifestyle, such as continuous mobility of people and goods.

When we deal with the (food) production facilities you introduce as an infrastructure, we need to ask who is our end user? It is problematic to only focus on humans; we should also consider other intelligencies including the plant, vegetable, microbial or animal intelligence, since such production infrastructure could potentially boost new ecosystems or microclimates for other species to thrive. At the same time, the same technologies we would require implementing this productive infrastructure could be considered another "species" which enhances or optimizes production and therefore affect ways of human living and interaction in unprecedented ways. Such a model starts to describe a novel civic infrastructure that is relevant to humans, but also to other species or entities. Considering plants, vegetables, robots, machines, meaning diverse cultural or technological others is a strong manifesto for the future infrastructure of the city.

Rafael Luna:
What you're proposing with this project might change the biodiversity of a city or allow for a new biodiversity. Another layer to the project might take a landscape urbanism approach to density in Australian cities. Farming as landscape urbanism could structure the city to bring biodiversity corridors into the urban fabric that moves from the rural fringe all the way into the centre, tying into your architectural typologies.

John Doyle:
We didn't consider biodiversity in the city as we wanted it to be as intensely occupied and productive as possible. By intensifying the city, we free the landscape outside its boundaries for rewilding, replacing cattle grazing which is currently what most agricultural land is used for in Australia. Perhaps can consider a scenario where we can have both?

Graham Crist:
The project continues to be relevant. Just when we were talking about density and cities, we ran into Covid-19, and everyone was talking about social distancing. Then just as we are talking about food production, half our country is being flooded and agricultural production is being destroyed. We're now learning where food comes from because we can see agricultural land under water or on fire. One of the most radical impacts could be to unravel the whole logistical system which separates production and consumption. We think the social impact of being where things are produced is quite subtle but profound.

John Doyle:
People go crazy in Australia about density in cities. We decided not to touch existing housing to acknowledge the circumstances of the city and in some ways force pockets of extremely high levels of density. It makes the proposition more radical by highlighting the discrepancy between very low levels of housing density and very high levels of productive density. Some of the interventions have one storey housing sitting on two-hectare sites right next to a tower of productive program. The project is also a polemical proposition around the absurdly low levels of housing density in Australian cities.

Areti Markopoulou:
The idea of connecting food production with concepts of density is very interesting. In Barcelona, we have been working on a similar project which transforms existing building terraces to farming and green spaces. One of the main things that we realised is that administrations were not really interested in the data of food production from this project, but they were interested in the qualitative impacts of these proposals. For example, if you green the roof of a building, how does it affect the internal micro-climate? How do neighbours interact? when suddenly there is a new open space within the building? The project was a demonstration that contributed to discussions on reprogramming terraces and now there is a regulation that provides financial support for the transformation of building groups in Barcelona. This support is not available to all buildings, only buildings that are able to be transformed, but it's interesting to see how such initiatives can creat an opportunity for a new approach in the city.

Peyman Akhgar:
It's very interesting that you mentioned the potential for household production within the city. In Australia it is very common for households to have some kind of small-scale agricultural production. Most of Australia's cities are made up of low-density suburbs comprised of single detached housing with large lots and lots of open area that can be used for planting.

Rafael Luna:
How would this project be implemented? Would this end up being from the private sector or the public sector? If it's from the public sector, it might end up being about the creation of planning or building codes to allow for the future implementation of these typologies over government owned land or infrastructural right of ways. In the project, most of the interventions appear on private land. How could we mediate between the public interest and private development. For example, perhaps every new building needs to have 30% agricultural production?

Graham Crist:
You're right. Nearly all allocated land is privately owned. So isn't a government enterprise, such as rezoning land. It is just creating the conditions where enterprise could do this just like it currently does outside of the city.

Antony Moulis:
For me the most provocative aspect is the idea that people's diet could change. It sits outside architecture, but it promotes what in government terms would be called a 'preventative health strategy'. The project argues that there is a direct relationship between architecture and the health of citizens.

John Doyle:
We see diet as a planning problem, and more specifically, a land use problem.

Areti Markopoulou:
We should also ask whether food should be grown using traditional approaches. We should look at alternative approaches to agricultural production, beyond hydroponics. At the Tallinn Architecture Biennale that we have co-curated with Lydia Kallipoliti, we collaborated with a number of architects and researchers to promote and propose ideas such as new breeding centres for future protein, like crickets. Crickets are thought to be a source of future protein. Other projects

explored the integration of algae into building components, taking advantage of photosynthetic activity in solar exposure to provide photo mediation, air filtration and food, such as spirulina. Another project in the Tallinn Architecture Biennale rethought the kitchen as a productive space of nutrients to feed other systems such as fertilizer to our garden or collect the organic waste that can become energy or new materials for future construction. This introduces a new model of what the domestic space of a kitchen is and how it can contribute to a building metabolism, rather than simply be a place to process and consume food.

Rafael Luna:
In the project chapter, you only mention fruit, vegetables, grains and legumes. The project doesn't include meat production.

John Doyle:
I think it was more of an ethical concern for us. We aren't ruling it out of the diet completely, but we didn't want to condone high-density animal rearing. While it isn't included in the project, we have in the past looked at lab grown meat production. This technology is rapidly evolving. In the time it has taken us to complete the project, lab grown meat has gone from science fiction to a commercial reality in some cities. It's almost economically viable and particularly in places where meat is scarce. Again, this raises the interesting question of what a lab grown meat production typology would look like?

Graham Crist:
As urban designers, if we propose to the city that you can either have a hundred storey sheds on every block or you can give up meat. I know which would be less controversial. Nothing triggers Australians more than talking about meat.

Rafael Luna:
If we think about this from a macro-economic perspective, Australia is a major global food producer. These proposals don't just impact Melbourne, but also Australia as a food producer. One of the problems we face for food production is the global shortage of fertilizer. Perhaps a future line of investigation is other forms of production that support agriculture. What if you start looking at the production of fertilizer in the city rather than the production of food itself? Could the production of food end up being not the actual growth of vegetation, but the means of producing vegetation?

Graham Crist:
Sure, but would you rather live next door to a fertilizer factory or a tomato farm?

John Doyle:
We pump a lot of nutrients back into aquifers and ocean environments. There is the potential to harvest food waste but also bodily waste. The city is already a fertilizer plant, we just don't capture and sell it. It is a very good point, and one we haven't really considered in this project. Food waste alone accounts for a huge percentage of agricultural production. A future iteration of this project might consider how waste recovery infrastructure is integrated into these urban and architectural typologies.

Areti Markopoulou:
New urban planning based around production allows the growth of food and repurpose of waste, as well as it contributes to renewable energy production. Organic waste can be transformed into biodegradable construction materials. By bringing production back into cities, projects like these can also produce biodiversity. I think it's incorrect to think that a breeding centre or a plant growing centre is an enclosed factory. I like that one of your proposed typologies looks like a village, another is totally sealed from view, and another one which is somehow semi-transparent. However, if we start to bring crops into the city or animals, then we have to allow for other species, particularly pollinators and birds. As you mention in the chapter, if we grow food in the city, we will have odors. So how do we plan for these multi species to inhabit while protecting humans from undesirable effects such as smells?

Antony Moulis:
In your experience, are city governments and politicians more receptive to a radical step or incremental evolution? What have you seen in response to these two approaches?

Areti Markopoulou:
If we really want to provide a solution to the current urban challenges of production and consumption, we need to somehow be as radical as John and Graham are in their proposal. But that is not the reality in terms of policy making in Europe. Current European policy is much more interested in enabling micro-farming in the city and on the periphery of the city. They are not so interested in the idea of huge infrastructures for massive production. I think this is interesting because it breaks this centralised model of mass production. It has the potential to involve people, users and citizens in the process of producing food at smaller localized scales. It might not be so effective in terms of amounts and quantities of what we produce, but it does foment a different culture for living in the built environment. It's more evolutionary rather than revolutionary. But it's probably something very important if we all understand and accept that it's not just policy and infrastructure that needs to change but also habits and behaviors.

John Doyle:
Food and food production is traditionally controlled by the interests of capital, as well as policy makers, economists and agricultural scientists. We are interested in how design can reimagine and research possible food futures.

Areti Markopoulou:
Design is a powerful combination of thought and action. It isn't only a tool to rethink and to question different processes, stereotypes, problematics, but it's also a tool for action. So, creative design is more necessary than ever. We need to innovate. We need to bring to the table novel solutions and novel ways of doing things because we are at a critical moment and there is no way back.

URBAN PRODUCTION FUTURES

This book imagines architecture's relationship with problematic futures. Architectural design is always dealing with future conditions, while responding to immediate problems. The projects in this book explore the latent possibilities present in the cities we live in, to project possible alternative future cities. These projects imagine those possibilities without forecasting one trajectory, and they do so at scales ranging from the house, to the urban precinct to the metropolitan territory. The intention has been to carefully observe an existing context and depart from it based on clearly traceable models and data. The purpose of design in responding to a context is to provide an environmental catalyst that could trigger multiple scenarios and to model them spatially. The designs of these projects make concrete a suite of scenarios for using urban space and land more productively.

The design process here has been to experiment with the everyday urban fabric of three cities and to inject it with more uses. These experiments attempt to see what can be achieved by an architectural or urban intervention of productive program. This ranges from domestic scale micro-enterprise, to an entire urban region co-opted to agricultural production. Each end of this scale infers an intensification of production at the scale of the precinct. These design experiments cannot be verified for their productive capacity but they can demonstrate the spatial implications of their moves, and they can elaborate the urban capacity already present. They are also set up to be partially implemented. That is, they imagine a scenario which may affect transformation if not fully realised. These experiments are triggered by observation of the urban environments of Brisbane, Seoul and Melbourne but they are applicable to each other and potentially to other cities. They are open propositions that suggest a series of potential outcomes. They also suggest infrastructures and actions by a range of other fields including planners, economists, and policy makers. They necessarily demand a wider public debate.

Embedded in these projects is an advocacy for more production in cities: the value of making things within a city, and much closer to where things are consumed. The designs give these notions scale and form. In many ways the demonstrated implications are modest in form, and transformative in the operations of cities and their economies.

The house, the warehouse, workshop or factory which already represent a productive capacity of the city are amplified or re-tooled for contemporary conditions.

The experiments use as their departure point everyday observations of the city, and technologies or trends that are presently available. The domestic and precinct scales document and make accelerated projections of present conditions in Brisbane and Seoul. The territorial project speculates on a bigger scale and therefore infers a more distant future, yet its components are realizable as a single precinct block. All the projects are based on existing urban phenomena that are already happening in spontaneous, informal and privately funded modes. They do not infer a re-planning of their cities but contribute an understanding of the agency of design in re-wiring or re-tooling urban structures. They suggest how design may shape and intensify trajectories of change that are already taking place. The cities in which the projects' experiments are based are highly regulated, with comprehensive building codes, zoning and planning requirements. In these contexts, the temptation to radically depart from or ignore the limitations imposed by the city's codes have instead given way to the questions: What is possible within the framework of codes as they exist? What adjustments to the codes are required to realise a productive scenario?

One of the key results of these experiments is that its radical aspect has less to do with breaking rules, with exuberant formal expression, and more to do with issues of scale and flexible use. Change is radical if there is enough of it. Enacted at scale these proposals have potential to fundamentally remake the city and its economies. In considering these propositions with the dialogue participants contained in this book, it has become clear that global change is accelerating and that many of the ideas explored through the projects are already happening and have been part of some everyday environments for some time. Urban change is ineludible and more rapid, than built architecture. [6.1]. A practice of constant speculation and experimentation is necessary to catch up, respond, and accommodate unknown futures.

6.1 The projects are the acceleration of existing urban conditions.

Architecture as infrastructure: Urbanism as a scaffold

Key to the framing of this design research is the idea of *architectural urbanism*, across varied scales: house, precinct, and territory. In these projects architecture performs not only as a single, independent object or container, but equally as a kind of infrastructure or scaffold, supporting productive events and activities.

Conceiving the projects at different scales demonstrate how infrastructures can be created for global cities and used to achieve more sustainable urban environments. Infrastructure conventionally refers to large-scale phenomena operating at the territorial scale and beyond. In this work infrastructure is re-scaled to consider the individual building or the local street block as urban infrastructure. The distinction between architecture and infrastructure does not apply when architectural elements themselves function as a type of supportive urban element. The domestic fence in Brisbane serves the house, allowing it to become more productive, and creating a context for commercial exchange or for greater possibilities of neighbourhood engagement. [6.2]. The suburb reconceived as a walkable 15-minute city[1], rather than a place of car movements, means each architectural intervention becomes active in forming that rescaled system. Each project provides an immediate site specific solution, but its effect is traceable across a much larger scale.

The architectural objects of these projects are consistently outwardly focused, with ambitions beyond themselves, whose value is measured in their

6.2 The Brisbane domestic fence becomes an infrastructural element that supports production.

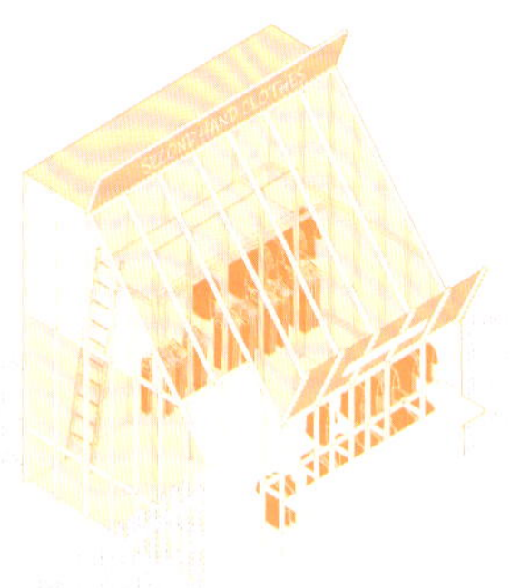

6.3 The Australian suburb has commonalities with Asian cities through its rapid expansion and capacity for adaptation and change.

6.4 Adaptability can occur through the augmentation and accesorisation of the building, and through similar operations at the territorial scale.

impact on the city. The contribution of the research is in developing architectural approaches that sit within existing fabrics, and span from informal makers through to large-scale industrial producers.

Incremental adaptability

A trait common to the cities considered in these projects, and more broadly cities in the Asia–Pacific region, is their capacity to morphologically adapt in radically different ways and at vastly different scales. The rapidly urbanising environments of Asia's cities have demonstrated a kind of *collective ingenuity* manifested through various acts of informal urbanism. The speed at which many cities through Southeast Asia, and particularly China, have grown over the last three decades has been astonishing, and is accompanied by informal adaptations. While the general perception of the Australian suburb is of a highly homogenous and regulated entity, a finer scaled review shows a significant amount of untapped potential in the form of unused space, and flexibility for rapid adaptability. [6.3]. What the projects reveal is that the potential for production in the Australian urban landscape is larger because of its loose low density. The key to this is the progressive, incremental, intensification and *tightening* of the Australian suburbs as a means of capitalising on their latent productive potential.

Adaptability is a form of evolution associated with *traditions* within a city context. Melbourne, Seoul and Brisbane are each cities which embraced the modern project, and its erasure or remaking of whole environments under the forces of colonialism or vast upheaval. [6.4]. Aldo Rossi's evolutionary approach outlined in *The Architecture of the City*[2], by contrast, situates urban artifacts in a continuum of form progressively adapting to changes of function. Urban forms survive change and transformation of use over time and despite the growth of the city. Our projects encourage, paradoxically, the unearthing, or even the authoring, of traditions of remaking within the established boundaries of these cities, advocating their evolution and building on what already exists.

Adaptability confronts designers with a foregrounding of the existing and the ad hoc or undesigned. This process though, particularly in the rapidly growing urban and suburban environments of the Asia–Pacific, is already occurring at speed. Adapted spaces take forms that we might ignore as banal. As Jeremy Till notes[3], the ubiquitous English Georgian house is easily adapted. A simple arrangement of similar rooms around a stair, allows for varied futures uses. We have explored simple adaptations of the suburban Brisbane house through tiny additions, infills and edge treatments. We have explored these ideas through three scales and locations of projects, through the adaptability of the suburban house, the augmentation of generic commercial buildings in Seoul and the potential of simple infill existing brownfield sites and low-intensity agricultural land at the metropolitan scale.

Adapting a city necessitates a degree of organisational looseness. Unlike functional specifics of modernity looseness accommodates unplanned uses and users over time. In the book *Supertight*, this condition is described as architectural overlapping. These design projects develop tools and strategies, and identify functional ambiguities within the city that support—and catalyse—multiple possible outcomes including the introduction of manufacturing programs.

The thesis shared by the three projects in this book is the necessity of de-zoning cities to inject more productive activity into the urban environment. New areas of manufacturing can be found within urban boundaries, avoiding the consumption of new territory. The extreme separation of food consumption from production is an example. In the case of urban agriculture for Melbourne, food production can take place far closer to home (instead of venturing far beyond it) by identifying ambiguous urban gaps. Blurring specific zones makes for more *mixité:* residential areas can become places to explore economic and entrepreneurial creativity, and startups can be launched from the kitchen table. In the case of Brisbane, we discussed how private properties can be reconsidered as sites of microscale production through design. As in the case of Seoul, highly mixed areas can bring different design languages together, generating a new aesthetic for the urban environment.

The relaxing of planning zones, the broadening of mixed-use zones and the creation of very fine grain specific zones are each strategies to overcome the dispersion of urban production. Each of these could be approached with an understanding of the benefits to returning production to the city, at tiny and large industrial scales.

The task of urban planning as limiting density and segregating uses is now superseded and is reconsidered where we are designing manufacturing enterprise back into cities. In places where children

6.5 Yoyogi park in Tokyo provides an example of how a space can be reused and adapted for multiple uses and activities.

have no idea of how food is grown and their parents could never walk to work, the discipline of city planning should facilitate and foster urban density and functional diversity. Such an agenda might stipulate minimum uses and minimum densities. The design projects here provide architectural manifestations of such possibilities, rather than the policies which determine them.

If the 20th century was defined, in part, by mass production, the 21st century will be the era of mass customization. New digital production technologies suggest more individualised tailoring of products and services. Gig economies, individual micro-enterprises, digital nomads working remotely, micro and block chain investments, and the access economy of rental products reflect the best and worst of this. These developments suggest a wealth of decentralised activities at the local level[4], which necessitate the rapid adaptability and alteration of the urban environment. The projects in this book explore the ways in which the city is being adapted to support the evolution of these economies. By identifying looseness, or opportunities for evolution, we provide a *cushion* in the city, a gap that the individual can *fill in* and create room to make their own physical environment. The agency of the individuals and communities to adjust their own environment fit-for-purpose is a strategy of sustainability that allows for the continual reuse of the city without the need for the urban environment to be completely remade each time. These actions bring a resilience to the city. While making the designs the world experienced major global crises and conflict—including war and pandemic. The consequences of these shifts in our closely linked resource network are enormous. A sustainable response means adaptation and adjustments rather than remaking afresh or abandoning. This book suggests a series of strategies for the adaptability of cities, which have been made visible through spatial design.

We have discovered in our cities the potential in these places for architectural ingenuity to make adjustments for a radically new city that stitches productive activities into the urban environment. While this research is highly specifically and focused on particularly places, scales, and types, the ambition of this research is its transfer to other cities and local contexts. The expectation is that Seoul, Brisbane, and Melbourne represent a series of test cases, a field of action, but the conclusions can be adopted elsewhere, shared, and reapplied.

The Value of a Productive City

For Cerdà[5], urbanisation was the network of all things involved in the production and consumption of the city. This conception of urbanisation underpins the formation of contemporary cities in 19th century. In the 21st century it seems we have excluded a large portion of that network from consideration. A straightforward understanding of the value of these projects is in reconciling present-day cities with a 19th century understanding of the complete urban system.

The project questions the separation in our developed cities, between the spaces in the central business districts (for producing services and consuming entertainment), suburbs (for consumption) and the global hinterland beyond, where goods, food, energy, and other consumables are produced to supply populations. While this division deepened in the late 20th and early 21st centuries, the COVID-19 pandemic and its supply crises laid bare economic problems within these structures. Today, the detachment of the things we consume from where they are produced shows negative social, economic, and environmental effects concerning isolation, waste, and carbon footprint that require attention.

Until all production is automated, people will continue to be employed in production. The segregation between those who work to produce goods and food, and those employed in knowledge economies presents a number of issues. While this is problematic as a form of segregation within a city, it is increasingly a global segregation of goods produced in low-wage nations and consumed in developed economies. This presents a fragile system of trade that is highly susceptible to the environmental and geo-political shocks we have seen in the last few years. Worse, it is a system of entrenched exploitation and inequality, in which the dislocation of workforces from consumption sites has led to economic gain for a small number of people. As the world transitions into the fourth industrial revolution, characterised by the digitalisation and decentralisation of clean production, this separation can be reconsidered. This research takes new technologies and subsequent economies as a catalyst for the revaluation of urban environments as productive-consumptive spaces. Underpinning this catalyst is the position that by visualising and spatialising the capacity for our cities to house sufficient production to match consumption, we demonstrate a future in which the inequities of this separation might be addressed. Architectural and urban strategies operate spatially, not directly in the political or financial sphere. Nonetheless, such strategies can act as agents of change by demonstrating new possibilities beyond the superseded image of the dirty industrial city.

Separating productive and consumptive spaces has also exacerbated the climate crisis by inflating the energy needed for consumption. It is an effect contrary to its intent: relocating manufacturing away from the city was a strategy to alleviate pollution in the urban environment. There are social benefits to placing consumers and producers in the same territory—placing them under the same environmental regulations. Such regulatory mechanisms are beyond the scope of these projects, yet they highlight the spatial advantages of mixité which have powerful social and environmental implications.

The impacts of expanding production into cities are considerable, and they are explored through design at various scales in three cities. Blending production and consumption (work and leisure) adds to the safety of neighborhood, improves urban walkability and the wellbeing of people living in the city. It generates opportunities for economic stimulation involving people, businesses, and governments in new ways, reshaping informal and formal economies. The expansion of production in the urban context reshapes populations, altering the composition of city life and its economies. These adaptive processes can occur from bottom-up engagement at micro scale, as well as very large enterprise. It infers greater engagement in the processes that make our cities.

Finally, these design strategies instrumentalise production within cities as a tool for rethinking the role of architecture and urban design. The 20th century decline of mass industry in developed urban economies has been overwhelmingly geared towards replacement with residential, leisure and commercial program. It is difficult to imagine alternative models to this. The reintroduction of industry and agriculture into a city provides an irritant for the reconceptualisation of the city. In responding to this prompt, it has become necessary to develop new architectural and urban types that loosen the relationship between the domestic, the commercial, and the industrial. The diagram of the city has become re-organised where the home is no longer becoming exclusively the domain of consumption and distant from the goods of that consumption. The projects have only begun to unpack the logistical and infrastructural effects of these proposals, though the designs described in this book certainly uncover and visualise the questions. They provide food for thought on future architectural and urban inventions.

Endnotes

1. For example https://www.15minutecity.com/.
2. Aldo Rossi, The Architecture of the City (L'architettura della città), Oppositions Books, 1984 (originally published Padova 1966).
3. Jeremy Till, Tatjana Schneider, Flexible Housing, Routledge, London, 2016.
4. While this is the experience on the ground, we acknowledge that the liberty of the consumer has been facilitated through the massive consolidation of economic power within the hands of a few companies and individuals. In this sense, in the 21st century, the global economy is more centralised than ever before.
5. Refer Ildefons Cerdà , Plan of the Eixample development in Barcelona (1859), commonly known as the Cerdà Plan.

CREDITS AND ACKNOWLEDGEMENTS

Image Credits

1.1 - Housing in London. (London: A Pilgrimage.) Wood Engraving. Gustave Doré. 1870.

1.2 - Single use zoning in the City of Melbourne. Map. Department of Transport and Planning. 2022.

1.3 - Broadacre City Frank Lloyd Wright. (The Disappearing City.) Drawing. Frank Lloyd Wright. 1932.

1.4 - Delhi. Photo. Photograph by Varun Shiv Kapur. 2012.

1.5 - The *Ever Given* disaster. Photo. From NASA JSC ISS image library. 2021

1.6 - Production outside of the city. Photo. Photographed by Alan Zomerfeld. 2006.

1.7 - Urban context of West End, Brisbane. Photo. Photograph by Anjanette Hudson. 2022.

2.1 - Shop under a detached house in West End, Brisbane. Photo. Photograph by Anjanette Hudson. 2022.

2.2 - Seongsu Production Urbanism. Photo. Photograph by John Doyle. 2023.

2.3 - Suburbs of Melbourne. Photo. Photograph by Graham Crist. 2023.

2.4 - The cataloguing of production accessories. Loose Accessories for a Tight Urbanity by PRAUD. Installation at the Making Tightness Exhibition. Photographed by Jonathon Griggs. 2021.

2.5 - High density agriculture. Growing Tight Food by RMIT Architecture. Installation at the Making Tightness Exhibition. Photograph by Jonathon Griggs 2021.

2.6 - Large scale future visions. Kenzo Tange Master Plan for Reconstruction of Skopje City Center. Photograph of model. Osamu Murai. 1965.

2.7- Process of adaptation and adjustment. Rasquachismo Series, Vietnam. Photographed by Archie Pizzini. 2018.

2.8 - Spatial and formal propositions developed. Graham Crist at the Making Tightness symposium at Melbourne Design Week 2021. Photographed by John Doyle. 2021.

2.9 - Preliminary design proposal. Digital rendering of UQ installation for the Making Tightness Exhibition. Design by Phorm Architecture. Design with Silvia Micheli and Antony Moulis. Produced by Lara Rann and Thomas Webster. 2021.

3.1 - Timber fence of a detached house in West End, Brisbane. Photograph by Anjanette Hudson. 2022.

3.2 - A residential house with dormant fence line. Photograph by Anjanette Hudson. 2022.

3.3 - Dormant edges in West End, Brisbane. Photograph by Anjanette Hudson. 2022.

3.4 - Axonometric map of a Brisbane suburb characterised with dormant fence lines. Computer drawing. Produced by Lily Éire Parsons. 2022.

3.5 - Street vendor, West End, Brisbane. Photo. Photograph by Antony Moulis. 2020.

3.6 - Street plant nursery and shop, West End, Brisbane. Photograph by Anjanette Hudson. 2022.

3.7 - Bike repair station, Dutton Park, Brisbane. Computer Drawing. Produced by Lily Éire Parsons. 2022.

3.8 - Bike repair station, Dutton Park, Brisbane. Photograph by Lily Éire Parsons. 2020.

3.9 - A local bookstore, Bardon, Brisbane. Computer Drawing. Produced by Lily Éire Parsons. 2022.

3.10 - A local bookstore, Bardon, Brisbane. Photograph by Lily Éire Parsons. 2020.

3.11 - Plastic recycling, Toowong, Brisbane. Computer Drawing. Produced by Lily Éire Parsons. 2022.

3.12 - Plastic recycling, Toowong, Brisbane. Photograph by Lara Rann. 2020.

3.13 - Fridge and plants for sale, Taringa, Brisbane. Photograph by Lara Rann. 2020.

3.14 - Fridge and plants for sale, Taringa, Brisbane. Computer drawing. Produced by Lily Éire Parsons. 2022.

3.15 - Design strategies for a second-hand clothes shop and a bike repair workshop. Computer drawing. Produced by Ivan Ling and Lily Éire Parsons. 2022.

3.16 - Design strategy for a bike repair workshop located in a suburban street. Drawing and photo collage. Produced by Lily Éire Parsons. 2022.

3.17 - Transforming a dormant suburb in a productive site. Computer drawing. Produced by Lily Éire Parsons. 2022.

3.18 - Installation model — 2021 Melbourne Design Week. Design by Phorm Architecture. Design with Silvia Micheli and Antony Moulis. Produced by Lara Rann and Thomas Webbster. 2021.

3.19 - Detailed drawings - productive elements. Computer drawing. Design by Phorm Architecture. Design with Silvia Micheli and Antony Moulis. Produced by Kelly Nortje. 2022.

3.20 - Installation model — 2021 Melbourne Design Week. Physical model. Design by Phorm Architecture. Design with Silvia Micheli and Antony Moulis. Produced by Lara Rann and Thomas Webster. 2021.

3.21 - Installation model — 2021 Melbourne Design Week. Physical model. Design by Phorm Architecture. Design with Silvia Micheli and Antony Moulis. Produced by Lara Rann and Thomas Webster. 2021.

3.22 - Installation model — 2021 Melbourne Design Week. Physical model. Design by Phorm Architecture. Design with Silvia Micheli and Antony Moulis. Produced by Lara Rann and Thomas Webster. 2021.

3.23 - Detailed drawings — productive elements. Computer drawing. Design by Phorm Architecture. Design with Silvia Micheli and Antony Moulis. Produced by Kelly Nortje. 2022.

3.24 - Longitudinal section—Extending the productive edge. Computer drawing. Design by Phorm Architecture. Design with Silvia Micheli and Antony Moulis. Produced by Kelly Nortje. 2022.

3.25 - Axonometric view—Extending the productive edge. Computer drawing. Design by Phorm Architecture. Design with Silvia Micheli and Antony Moulis. Produced by Kelly Nortje. 2022.

4.1 – Streetview in Seongsu-dong. Photo. Taken by PRAUD. 2020.

4.2 – The Social Maps of Seoul. Map. Seoul Solution. 2021.

4.3 – Building Function Mapping. Drawing. Produced by PRAUD and Hongik University led by Dongwoo Yim. 2019.

4.4 – Photo of Shoe Street in Seongsu-dong. Photo. Taken by PRAUD. 2019.

4.5 – Urban Morphologies. Drawing. Produced by PRAUD and Hongik University led by Dongwoo Yim. 2019.

4.6 – Urban Factories. Drawing. Produced by PRAUD. 2019.

4.7 – Attachments. Photos. Taken by PRAUD. 2020.

4.8 – Productive Elements. Drawing. Produced by PRAUD. 2021.

5.24 – Devon Meadows Agricultural Facility. Isometric Drawing. RMIT Architecture: John Doyle, Graham Crist, Sally-Anne Ciantar, Hepeng Miao, Gabriel Lim, Jinal Gandhi, Kang Samanchit, Jazz Pedder, Duresha Situge, Albany Flanagan, Emma Goodieson, Marcus Hall. 2021.

5.26 – Devon Meadows Agricultural Facility. Architectural Rendering. RMIT Architecture: John Doyle, Graham Crist, Sally-Anne Ciantar, Hepeng Miao, Gabriel Lim, Jinal Gandhi, Kang Samanchit, Jazz Pedder, Duresha Situge, Albany Flanagan, Emma Goodieson, Marcus Hall. 2021.

5.26 – Devon Meadows Agricultural Facility. Architectural Rendering. RMIT Architecture: John Doyle, Graham Crist, Sally-Anne Ciantar, Hepeng Miao, Gabriel Lim, Jinal Gandhi, Kang Samanchit, Jazz Pedder, Duresha Situge, Albany Flanagan, Emma Goodieson, Marcus Hall. 2021.

5.27 – Brooklyn Agricultural Factory. Isometric Drawing. RMIT Architecture: John Doyle, Graham Crist, Sally-Anne Ciantar, Hepeng Miao, Gabriel Lim, Jinal Gandhi, Kang Samanchit, Jazz Pedder, Duresha Situge, Albany Flanagan, Emma Goodieson, Marcus Hall. 2021.

5.28 – Brooklyn Agricultural Factory. Architectural Rendering. RMIT Architecture: John Doyle, Graham Crist, Sally-Anne Ciantar, Hepeng Miao, Gabriel Lim, Jinal Gandhi, Kang Samanchit, Jazz Pedder, Duresha Situge, Albany Flanagan, Emma Goodieson, Marcus Hall. 2021.

5.29 – North Melbourne Agriculture Sites. Architectural Rendering. RMIT Architecture: John Doyle, Graham Crist, Inez Kozak & Ayana Lokhandwala. 2022.

5.30 – Vertical Farm Typologies. Isometric Drawings. RMIT Architecture, John Doyle, Graham Crist, Nikola Sormaz, Audrey Avianto, Joelle Samaan, Yiqiao Zhao, Christine Yau, Chupei Zhang, Tsz Chan. 2022.

5.31 – North Melbourne Farm Tower. Architectural Rendering. Laura Mártires, RMIT Architecture: John Doyle, Graham Crist, Joshua Corban-Banks, Kaveen, Ayana Lokhandwala, William Hartawan, Trisha Karkhanis, Kaveen Gallage, Aoxiang Zheng. 2022.

5.32 – North Melbourne Farm Tower. Section Drawing. RMIT Architecture: John Doyle, Graham Crist, & Ayana Lokhandwala. 2022.

5.33 – North Melbourne Farm Tower. Exploded Isometric Drawing. RMIT Architecture: John Doyle, Graham Crist, & William Hartawan. 2022.

5.34 – North Melbourne Farm Tower. Architectural Rendering. Laura Mártires, RMIT Architecture: John Doyle, Graham Crist, Joshua Corban-Banks, Kaveen, Ayana Lokhandwala, William Hartawan, Trisha Karkhanis, Kaveen Gallage, Aoxiang Zheng. 2022.

5.35 – North Melbourne Farm Tower. Architectural Rendering. Laura Mártires, RMIT Architecture: John Doyle, Graham Crist, Joshua Corban-Banks, Kaveen, Ayana Lokhandwala, William Hartawan, Trisha Karkhanis, Kaveen Gallage, Aoxiang Zheng. 2022.

5.36 – North Melbourne Farm Tower. Architectural Rendering. Laura Mártires, RMIT Architecture: John Doyle, Graham Crist, Joshua Corban-Banks, Kaveen, Ayana Lokhandwala, William Hartawan, Trisha Karkhanis, Kaveen Gallage, Aoxiang Zheng. 2022.

5.37 – North Melbourne Farm Tower. Architectural Rendering. Laura Mártires, RMIT Architecture: John Doyle, Graham Crist, Joshua Corban-Banks, Kaveen, Ayana Lokhandwala, William Hartawan, Trisha Karkhanis, Kaveen Gallage, Aoxiang Zheng. 2022.

5.38 – North Melbourne Farm Tower. Architectural Rendering. Laura Mártires, RMIT Architecture: John Doyle, Graham Crist, Joshua Corban-Banks, Kaveen, Ayana Lokhandwala, William Hartawan, Trisha Karkhanis, Kaveen Gallage, Aoxiang Zheng. 2022.

6.1 - Goods sale at the undercroft of a detached house, Brisbane. Photo. Photograph by Ivan Ling. 2020.

6.2 - Design strategy for a second-hand clothes shop. Computer drawing. Produced by Ivan Ling and Lily Éire Parsons. 2022.

6.3 - House in Tarneit. Photograph by Parth Nasit. 2023

6.4 - Seongsu Adaptations. Photograph by John Doyle. 2023

6.5 - Tight Density, Tight Familiarity, Overlapping City. Digital Photograph. Shiozaki Lab. 2019.

Acknowledgments

This book is the result of an international collaboration conducted between three research teams located at The University of Queensland School of Architecture, the architecture firm PRAUD, and RMIT University's School of Architecture and Urban Design (referred to throughout this book as the Productive Cities research team). The collaboration began after the 2019 Seoul Biennale of Architecture and Urbanism: Cities Exhibition, curated by PRAUD. This event challenged the contemporary state of dispersion, densities, accessibility, and approaches to sustainable economies. In 2020, the collaborators successfully applied for a grant from the Australia–Korean Foundation, an organisation established by the Australian Government's Department of Foreign Affairs and Trade, to promote bilateral cultural relations between Korea and Australia. We wish to thank the Australia–Korean Foundation for trusting and supporting the project underpinning this book.

As part of the grant, an itinerant design exhibition titled Making Tight was officially opened during Melbourne Design Week in March 2021 at the RMIT Design Hub Gallery. Three talks were held to discuss the propositions put forward by the research teams and their collaborators. We thank the team at the RMIT Design Hub Gallery for their support, and the Melbourne Design Week team and RMIT Architecture, led by Professor Vivian Mitsogianni, for their assistance. We thank the team of RMIT Architecture students who assisted with the exhibition. We also thank the following team of RMIT Architecture students who have contributed to this publication: Akshayan Parameswaran, Albany Flanagan, Alexandra Bennett, Andrew Wan Lun Chung, Angie Chan, Aoxiang Zheng, Arundhati Saxena, Ashlee Pukk, Audrey Avianto, Ayana Lokhandwala, Blake Hillebrand, Christine Yau, Chupei Zhang, Duresha Situge, Emma Goodieson, Gabriel Lim, Hepeng Miao, Inez Kozak, Jaskiran Kaur, Jazz Pedder, Jinal Gandhi, Jingtong Zhao, Jinyi Chen, Joelle Samaan, Joshua Corban-Banks, Kang Samanchit, Kaveen Gallage, Marcus Hall, Nadia Poppen, Nikola Sormaz, Prani Patton, Robin Chatterjee, Ronald Ching Ming Lau, Ruby Lang, Sally-Anne Ciantar, Touchthep Samanchit, Trisha Karkhanis, Tsz Chan, Viren Husin, William Hartawan, Yanlan Wu, Yiqiao Zhao.

The University of Queensland team would like to thank Phorm architecture + design for collaborating on the Making Tight exhibition, and principal Paul Hotston for his participation in the Melbourne Design Week event. In August 2021, Making Tight travelled to Brisbane to be displayed at The University of Queensland's Open Day. We wish to thank the (then) Head of the School of Architecture, Cameron Bruhn, for hosting the exhibition and Sam Butler and Sonya Brown from the Architecture Workshop for making it happen. We also thank the UQ Team of Ivan Ling, Kelly Nortje, Lily Éire Parsons, Lara Rann and Thomas Webster.

The Making Tight exhibition culminated in a final symposium in Seoul in November 2022 at the Domansa Urban Gallery. We would like to thank Domansa and its staff for hosting the symposium and acknowledge the support of the Australian Embassy in Seoul for their assistance with the event. We would also like to thank our colleagues in Seoul for attending and contributing to the live discussion.

The idea of converting the research outcomes into a co-authored book emerged in 2021. The editorial project benefitted from the assistance of our discussants, who have challenged our ideas and added to our theoretical propositions. A big thank you to Associate Professor Remi Ayoko from The University of Queensland Business School, Professor Revital [Tali] Hatuka from the Tel Aviv University, and Areti Markopoulou, Academic Director of the Institute for Advanced Architecture of Catalonia (IAAC), for their time and intellectual input that expanded our project's perspective.

Thank you to Gordon Goff from ORO for enthusiastically accepting our book proposal and working towards its realisation, and to The University of Queensland and RMIT Architecture for their support with the production of this book.

This book would have not been possible without the unconditional support of our families who have been so understanding and encouraging during the difficult COVID-19 disease pandemic.

Dr Silvia Micheli is a Senior Lecturer at The University of Queensland, Australia, where she researches and teaches contemporary design and history of architecture. She graduated from the Politecnico di Milano and defended her PhD, at the IUAV University in Venice. Micheli's design research focuses on the productive city and how small-scale projects can enhance functionality and livability in our communities. In 2021, Silvia co-designed the Blue Bower Pavilion, recipient of the Crossroads X Prize at the 2021 Seoul Biennale of Architecture and Urbanism. In 2018, she co-designed the multi-awarded residential building One Room Tower (2018) (Phorm architecture + design with Antony Moulis), a demonstration project for the densification of the city. Micheli has had a range of international collaborations with cultural institutions, such as the Alvar Aalto Foundation, Vitra Design Museum, Centre Pompidou, and MAXXI Museum (Rome). She is co-editor of the book *Italy/Australia: Postmodern Architecture in Translation* (URO, 2018) and is currently preparing a book on Italian postmodern architecture Paolo Portoghesi: Architecture between History, Politics and Media, to be published by Bloomsbury in 2023.

Dr Antony Moulis is Associate Professor in the School of Architecture at The University of Queensland, where he teaches and researches across architectural history and theory, urbanism, and design. His collaborative design research investigates resilience and micro-urbanism in the contemporary city with built and speculative projects featured in international journals such as Architecture Australia, The Architectural Review, GA Houses, and an invited installation at the 2021 Seoul Biennale of Architecture and Urbanism. This research includes the award-winning project One Room Tower (2018) (Phorm architecture + design with Silvia Micheli) located in inner-city Brisbane, and participation in the nationally based Water Sensitive Cities Cooperative Research Centre developing design strategies for flood resilient urban infrastructure. Moulis is also a critical commentator on architecture and international expert on Australian Modern Architecture. His recent works include the co-authored John Andrews: Architect of Uncommon Sense (Harvard University Press, 2023), the authored book Le Corbusier in the Antipodes: Art, Architecture and Urbanism (Routledge, 2021), and the co-edited 4-volume anthology, Le Corbusier: Critical Concepts in Architecture (Routledge, 2018).

Dr Peyman Akhgar, lecturer at Griffith University, was a 2022 Early Career Development Fellow in the School of Architecture at the University of Queensland. He graduated from Politecnico di Milano in 2016. While in Italy, he worked in award-winning architecture and urban design firms, gaining expertise in the field (2015). Starting his PhD in 2017 at The University of Queensland, he engaged in critical writing about everyday urbanism and design, space, place, people, and cultural identity. His writings have been extensively published in leading journals, such as the Journal of Architecture, Fabrications, and Architecture Australia Magazine, and he has presented his research at more than a dozen international conferences in Australia, New Zealand, France, Poland, and the United Kingdom. Akhgar has also coordinated undergraduate and postgraduate design and research courses at The University of Queensland focusing on retrofitting contemporary cities, resilient communities and place-making.

Dr Rafael Luna is co-founder of the architecture firm PRAUD and Senior Lecturer at the University of Technology Sydney. He received a Master of Architecture from the Massachusetts Institute of Technology (2010), and his PhD in Architecture from L'Accademia di architettura dell'Università della Svizzera italiana in Mendrisio (2022). Luna is the winner of the Architectural League Prize 2013, and his work has been exhibited at the Museum of Modern Art in New York, Venice Biennale, and Seoul Biennale. Luna was co-curator of the Cities Exhibition for the 2019 Seoul Biennale. He has professional experience from the offices of Toyo Ito and Associates, KPF, Ateliers Jean Nouvel, Martha Schwartz Partners, dECOI, Sasaki Associates, and Machado and Silvetti. He served as an assistant professor at Hanyang University between 2018 and 2022, previously teaching at the Rhode Island School of Design. His writings have been published in journals such as G+L, Topos, MONU, SPACE, IntAR Journal. Luna was a guest co-editor for AD magazine's September 2021 issue "Production Urbanism: The Meta-Industrial City." He is the co-author of the books I Want to Be Metropolitan (ORO, 2012) and the North Korean Atlas (Damdi, 2014).

Dongwoo Yim is co-founder of the architecture firm PRAUD and Assistant Professor at the Hongik University Graduate School of Architecture and Urban Design. He received his masters degree at Harvard University and a bachelor degree at Seoul National University. Yim is currently a PhD candidate at Università della Svizzera Italiana, Mendrisio. He is the winner of the Architectural League Prize 2013. He is the author of the books Pyongyang, and Pyongyang After (Hyosung Publishing, 2011), and (Un) Precedented Pyongyang (Actar, 2017), and co-author of North Korean Atlas (Damdi, 2014) and I Want to be Metropolitan (ORO, 2012). Yim's works have been exhibited worldwide including the Golden Lion-winning Korean Pavilion in Venice Biennale 2014, the Museum of Modern Art in New York, and DNA Galerie in Berlin. He has also held academic positions at the Rhode Island School of Design from 2011 through to 2017 and was a visiting assistant professor at Washington University in St. Louis in 2016. He was the curator of the installation Pyongyang Sallim and Letters to the Mayor: Seoul + Pyongyang at the 2017 Seoul Biennale of Architecture and Urbanism, and co-curator of the Cities Exhibition in the following biennale edition in 2019.

Dr Graham Crist is an Associate Professor in Architecture at RMIT University School of Architecture and Urban Design. He is the Program Director of the Master of Urban Design program and formerly the program director of the Master of Architecture in that school. He is the founding director of Melbourne-based architectural practice Antarctica Architects. Crist is the author, with John Doyle of Supertight: Models for Living and Making Culture in Dense Urban Environments (Actar, 2021), which focuses on the qualities of big cities in east Asia. A previous collaborative design project FARM HD examined the potential of very dense vertical agriculture in Hong Kong. Together, these projects pursue a wider interest in contribution of architectural design to reducing the human footprint of contemporary cities. Crist grew up and completed his undergraduate education in Perth, Western Australia—one of the most sprawled metropoles on Earth.

Dr John Doyle is an Associate Dean and Head of Architecture at RMIT University. He is a registered practising architect and partner at Common. Doyle's research practice uses architectural design tools to explore innovative models for urban design. Recently, his research has focused on rapid urbanisation in megacities throughout Asia. This research has developed a series of high-density urban models to address the challenges related to climate change, as well as equity, affordability, and food security. His work has been exhibited widely, including at the Shenzhen, Seoul, Rotterdam, Tallinn and Venice architecture biennales. He is the co-author of Supertight: Models for Living and Making Culture in Dense Urban Environments (Aktar, 2021). In 2022 he was awarded the RMIT Award for Research Excellence (Design)—Early Career Researcher.

Other contributors

Nina Rappaport is an architectural historian, curator, educator, and consultant. Her work focuses on industrial urbanism, encouraging urban production spaces, and the role of the factory worker. She is author of Vertical Urban Factory (Actar, 2015) and co-editor of Design of Urban Manufacturing (Routledge, 2020). Her exhibition, Vertical Urban Factory, has traveled to twelve cities since 2011. Her ongoing film project, A Worker's Lunch Box, features interviews with factory workers. Nina is Publications Director at the Yale School of Architecture. She has been a Visiting Professor at Politecnico di Torino and she teaches at the College of Public Architecture at Kean University in the United States.

Dr Oluremi (Remi) Ayoko is an Associate Professor of Management in the Business School at The University of Queensland. She is also a Senior Fellow of the Higher Education Academy (SFHEA) and the Convener/Co-Leader of the Next Generation of Workspaces Research Network at The University of Queensland. Ayoko's principal research interests include the physical work environment, territoriality, conflict, leadership, diversity, and teamwork. She has published in reputable journals, written several book chapters, and co-edited two books, including Organizational Behavior and the Physical Environment (Routledge, 2020). Ayoko is currently the Editor-in-Chief of the Journal of Management & Organization and sits on several journal editorial boards.

Dr Tali Hatuka is an architect, urban planner, and Associate Professor at Tel Aviv University. Hatuka is the Head and founder of the Laboratory of Contemporary Urban Planning and Design (LCUD) at Tel Aviv University and her work focuses on the urban realm and society (public space, conflicts, and technology) and urban development and city design (housing and industry). Hatuka graduated from the Faculty of Architecture and Town Planning at the Technion, Israel; she received a Master of Science in Urban Design from Edinburgh College of Art, Heriot-Watt University, in the United Kingdom; and a doctorate from the Technion in Isreal. She was a Fulbright Scholar and a Marie Curie Fellow in the Department of Urban Studies and Planning at MIT.

Areti Markopoulou is an architect, researcher, and urban technologist working at the intersection between architecture and digital technologies. She holds the position of Academic Director at IAAC in Barcelona and leads the Advanced Architecture Group. Her research and practice focus on redefining the architecture of cities through an ecological and technological spectrum combining design with biotechnologies, new materials, digital fabrication, and big data. She is the co-founder of the StudioP52 art residency and co-editor at Urban Next, a global network focused on rethinking architecture through the contemporary urban milieu. Markopoulou is project coordinator of several European Research-funded projects on topics including urban regeneration though data science, circular design and construction, and multidisciplinary education in the digital age.

Other Credits

ORO Editions
Publishers of Architecture, Art, and Design

Gordon Goff: Publisher

www.oroeditions.com

info@oroeditions.com

Published by ORO Editions.

Authors: Rafael Luna, Dongwoo Yim, John Doyle, Graham Crist, Silvia Micheli, Antony Moulis.

Book Design: Studio Unfold

Project Manager: Jake Anderson

10 9 8 7 6 5 4 3 2 1 First Edition

ISBN: 978-1-957183-64-0

Color Separations and Printing: ORO Editions Inc.

Printed in China

ORO Editions makes a continuous effort to minimize the overall carbon footprint of its publications. As part of this goal, ORO, in association with Global ReLeaf, arranges to plant trees to replace those used in the manufacturing of the paper produced for its books. Global ReLeaf is an international campaign run by American Forests, one of the world's oldest nonprofit conservation organizations. Global ReLeaf is American Forests' education and action program that helps individuals, organizations, agencies, and corporations improve the local and global environment by planting and caring for trees.